Emperors, Kings & Queens

Publisher and Creative Director: Nick Wells
Project Editor: Sara Robson
Picture Research: Victoria Lyle and Gemma Walters
Art Director: Mike Spender
Digital Design and Production: Chris Herbert
Layout Design: David Jones

Thanks to: Claire Walker and Anna Groves

This is a **STAR FIRE** book

STAR FIRE BOOKS
Crabtree Hall, Crabtree Lane
Fulham, London SW6 6TY
United Kingdom
www.star-fire.co.uk

Star Fire is part of The Foundry Creative Media Company Limited

07 09 11 10 08

1 3 5 7 9 10 8 6 4 2

ISBN 978-1-84451-814-2

A copy of the CIP data for this book is available from the British Library.

Printed in China

Author Biographies

Sonya Newland (author) has written on historical subjects from Ancient Egypt to the Second World War, the British monarchy to landmarks of the British Isles. She is currently undertaking a masters degree in Arthurian Studies in between her work as a writer and editor.

William Doyle (consultant) is a Professor of Early Modern History in the Department of Historical Studies at the University of Bristol, specializing in the history of eighteenth-century Europe. His books include *The Old European Order*, *The Oxford History of the French Revolution* and *The Ancient Regime* (2001). He has contributed hundreds of articles and reviews to numerous journals and publications.

Emperors, Kings & Queens

by Sonya Newland
Introduction by William Doyle

STAR FIRE

Contents

Introduction

For much of their history, most states in Europe have been monarchies. Only within living memory have republics come to outnumber them, and down to the First World War constitutional monarchs, who reign but do not rule, were the exception. For centuries beforehand, dynasties, not nation states, determined the map of Europe and the pattern of conflict. Kings and queens, emperors and empresses, held in their hands the fate of peoples.

For a thousand years there was only one emperor in Europe, and he was elected by the leading princes of Germany to head the enduring relic of the realms of Charlemagne, the Holy Roman Empire. But his power was very limited in a German federation comprising largely autonomous and often bitterly antagonistic

principalities. The real strength of the Austrian Habsburg who was almost invariably elected emperor lay in his hereditary lands along the Danube. When Emperor Francis II abdicated the imperial throne in 1806 he immediately took the title of Emperor Francis I of Austria to match the new imperial claims of Napoleon of France and the Russian tsar. In 1870 the King of Prussia would create a new German Empire, this time hereditary in his own house; and eight years later the British monarch's ministers would respond by declaring her Empress of India.

Most kings, however, never dreamed of upgrading their status in this way. They were happy if they were able to extend their hereditary dominions by conquest or more often by shrewd dynastic marriages. Even this sometimes failed. As the sixteenth century drew to a close, a number of dynasties disappeared and new ones emerged. The last Tudor monarch of England, Elizabeth I, left her realm to the Stuart king of Scotland. Assassination carried off the last Valois king of France and Henry IV inaugurated two centuries of rule by the house of Bourbon, which eventually occupied thrones in Spain and Italy too. In Russia the Romanovs emerged from the 'Time of Troubles' in the early seventeenth century to rule until the Bolshevik Revolution of 1917; while the rivalries of Nordic dynasties in Denmark and Sweden only ended with the establishment of a third kingdom in Norway in 1905. The most successful of all dynasties, the Habsburgs, ruled Spain (and even Portugal for a time) as well as their central European heartlands until the early eighteenth century. They retained many of the latter until the First World War – triggered by the murder of the heir to this collection of crowns.

the preceding century and a half had seen the steady rise of a new dynasty, the Hohenzollerns of Prussia, who came to rule most German-speaking lands before another century had gone by. By that time, too, Italy had been united into a single kingdom under the House of Savoy, Greece had a fragile monarchy, and Belgium had established a separate crown in the southern Netherlands.

There were many smaller kingdoms throughout this period whose importance was more transient. Most – though not all – were swallowed up by larger entities sooner or later. It has not been possible here to include all of these, or every ruler who wore a crown over four crowded centuries, or indeed to chart the often tangled and disputed dynastic relations between them, which repeatedly brought conflict and destruction to so many of their subjects. Not even all the children of the families who do appear can be listed. Many had more than a dozen offspring, and one is reputed to have fathered more than 300! The tragic complexity of dynastic interrelationships is symbolised by the way that three cousins – George V of Great Britain, William II of Germany and Nicholas II of Russia – found themselves in conflict during the First World War, a struggle that swept away forever the thrones of two of them. Yet most of the monarchs chronicled here mattered. Ruling by genetic chance irrespective of their abilities, it was they who made the great decisions, for better or worse, that dictated the course of European history over these centuries, and did much to shape the continent we know. Emperors are all long gone, but seven European states are still headed by kings and queens. They no longer wield real power; and perhaps that is why their fellow citizens show so little sign that they might prefer to live in republics.

Some ancient kingdoms also disappeared. Poland, once one of the most extensive realms in Europe, was partitioned out of existence by its neighbours in 1795, and its elective monarch pensioned off. The other elective crown, that of the Holy Roman Empire itself, followed 11 years later, swept away by the forces of the French Revolution that would eventually, after a number of disastrous restorations, leave France itself a republic. But within Germany

William Doyle

1600-1699

The House of Stuart

James I to William III

Sigismund III united himself with the Habsburgs through his marriages to the two daughters of Archduke Charles II of Austria.

Sigismund III (1566–1632)

KING OF POLAND (1587–1632)

House of Vasa

Sigismund was the son of the Swedish king John III but was elected to the Polish throne in 1587. Although Sweden was a Protestant country, Sigismund had been brought up a Catholic, and to secure the Swedish succession in 1594 he had agreed to support the country's prevalent Lutheranism. His later support of the Catholic counter-reformation saw a dramatic drop in Swedish favour and his uncle, Charles, in whose hands he had left the country when he accepted the Polish crown, began stirring up trouble. Sigismund was issued with an ultimatum that forbade him to rule Sweden from abroad. Rejection of this led to his overthrow in his native country. For all his professed devotion to Poland, Sigismund seems only to have used the country as a base from which to wage a campaign to regain Sweden; he formed several alliances to achieve this goal, most notably with the powerful Habsburgs. He did not succeed, and on his death his Polish title passed first to Ladislas IV, the eldest son from his first marriage to Anne of Austria, and then to John II, born to her sister and Sigismund's second wife, Constance.

Royal Connections

Cousin: Gustav II Adolf of Sweden *d. 1632* (❦ page 17)

Married

1. Anne of Austria *d. 1598*

2. Constance of Austria *d. 1631*

Children

Ladislas IV of Poland *d. 1648* (❦ page 25)

John II of Poland *d. 1672* (❦ page 32)

Christian IV (1577–1648)

KING OF DENMARK AND NORWAY (1588–1648)

House of Oldenburg

Christian IV left a mixed legacy from his 60-year reign. He is remembered as a cultured king, a lover of music and architecture, who founded many important buildings and towns, including Christiana – now Oslo. He also sought to improve international trade and founded the Danish East India Company, marking the early beginnings of Denmark's colonial empire.

Christian's personal life was rather less successful. His marriage to Anne Catherine of Brandenburg resulted in six children, including the future Frederick III. After Anne died Christian married Kirsten Munk. Although she bore him 12 more children, she was the subject of much intrigue and scandal at the Danish court, and was eventually discovered to have been conducting an affair. With Kirsten safely banished, Christian began his own affair with a former servant girl, Vibeke Kruse. The king's second wife and his mistress were bitter enemies and the feud continued – through their children – long after Christian's death.

This domestic upheaval was reflected in his foreign policy. Although the Kalmar War with Sweden brought victory for the Danish king in 1613, it made an enemy of a powerful neighbour. Sweden later came to Denmark's rescue after Christian made a disastrous intervention in the Thirty Years' War against Holy Roman Emperor Ferdinand II, but instead of building on the alliance Christian set about trying to reduce Swedish influence among the German states. The animosity culminated in the last years of his reign in the Torstensson Feud, in which Denmark was forced to cede some of its lands. Despite Christian's well-intentioned warmongering, by the end of his reign – just as the Peace of Westphalia concluded the Thirty Years' War – it was Sweden that had emerged as the great power among the Nordic countries.

Christian IV sought to extend Denmark's power through reforms in industry, commerce and the military.

Royal Connections

Brother-in-law: James I of England, Scotland and Ireland *d. 1625* (⚜ page 15)

Grandson: Christian V of Denmark and Norway *d. 1699* (⚜ page 43)

Married

1. Anne Catherine of Brandenburg *d. 1612*

2. Kirsten Munk *d. 1658*

Children

Frederick III of Denmark and Norway *d. 1670* (⚜ page 33)

Henry IV (1553–1610)

KING OF FRANCE (1589–1610)

House of Bourbon

Henry IV cut his teeth as ruler of Navarre, an independent kingdom straddling the Pyrenees. In 1513, the southern part of the region had been absorbed into the Kingdom of Spain, but the northern part remained independent until Henry nominally unified it with France.

His accession to the French throne was not easy. The Protestant Henry's marriage in 1572 to Margaret of Valois, sister of the French king Henry III, was ostensibly to bring accord to a region rife with religious unrest. But six days after the wedding the St Bartholomew's Day Massacre took place, in which thousands of French Protestant Huguenots were butchered. Henry himself was only saved by a swift – and insincere – conversion to Catholicism. He was held captive at the French court for four years before escaping and making his real sympathies known by joining forces against the French king. Even after his accession to the throne (on the assassination of the childless Henry III) and a permanent conversion to the Catholic faith in 1593, he spent years fighting the Catholic League to secure his kingdom.

The first French king of the Bourbon house, Henry IV endeared himself to his subjects by exercising a domestic restraint and concern for his people that was a welcome contrast to the selfish extravagance of the Valois monarchs who had preceded him. Among the most significant of his domestic policies was his religious tolerance, exercised most notably through the Edict of Nantes (1595), which granted the Huguenots political rights and officially ended years of civil war.

Having finally established a relative peace in his kingdom, Henry had his marriage to Margaret annulled and took a new wife, Marie de Medici. Marie provided him with six children, whose subsequent marriages saw Bourbon blood begin to mingle with that of seventeenth-century Europe's other dominant dynasties.

Royal Connections

Grandsons: Charles II of England, Scotland and Ireland *d. 1685* (❧ page 38),
James I of England, Scotland and Ireland *d. 1701* (❧ page 49),
Louis XIV of France *d. 1715* (❧ page 28)

Married

1. Margaret of Valois *d. 1615*
2. Marie de Medici *d. 1642*

Children

Louis XIII of France *d. 1643* (❧ page 16)
Elisabeth m. Philip IV of Spain *d. 1665* (❧ page 22)
Henrietta Maria m. Charles I of England, Scotland and Ireland *d. 1649* (❧ page 23)

Philip III (1578–1621)

KING OF SPAIN AND PORTUGAL (AS PHILIP II, 1598–1621)
House of Habsburg

Philip's father, Philip II, had been a pious but untrusting man. He eschewed the help of his ministers, fearing their ambition, and ruled his kingdom alone – with no small success. Philip III shared his father's religious devotion but lacked his leadership qualities. Preferring to spend his time enjoying lavish courtly entertainments, he left the running of the realm in the hands of his willing but inept favourite, Francisco Gómez de Sandoval y Rojas, the Duke of Lerma. By the time Philip IV came to the throne in 1621 the powerful and secure kingdom his grandfather had worked so hard to establish was virtually unrecognisable.

Royal Connections

Brother-in-law: Holy Roman Emperor Ferdinand II *d. 1637* (⚜ page 20)

Married

Margaret of Austria *d. 1611*

Children

Anne of Austria m. Louis XIII of France *d. 1643* (⚜ page 16)

Philip IV of Spain and Portugal *d. 1665* (⚜ page 22)

Maria Anna of Spain m. Holy Roman Emperor Ferdinand III *d. 1657* (⚜ page 26)

James I (1566–1625)

KING OF SCOTLAND (AS JAMES VI, 1567–1625),

KING OF ENGLAND AND IRELAND (1603–25)

House of Stuart

On her deathbed in 1603 the last Tudor monarch of England, Elizabeth I, named her 'cousin Scotland' as successor to her throne, and so it was that James VI of Scotland became James I of England. James's foreign policy was conciliatory. He concluded a peace with England's long-term enemy Spain while maintaining a good relationship with the Dutch, who were still fighting for independence from the Habsburgs. However, the marriage of his daughter Elizabeth to the German prince Frederick, the Elector Palatine, saw these fragile relationships break down. By the end of his reign he was at war with Spain again as his son and heir married a French princess.

In Scotland James had spent years establishing his authority over Church and State, but he found this sadly lacking when he moved to London. There parliament wielded a power over the monarch that James found humiliating. His resentment of this, and his increasingly vociferous belief in the 'Divine Right of Kings', sowed the seeds of the civil unrest that later brought his son's reign to such a violent end.

Royal Connections

Brother-in-law: Christian IV of Denmark and Norway *d. 1648* (✤ page 11)

Grandson: Charles II of England, Scotland and Ireland *d. 1685* (✤ page 38)

Married

Anne of Denmark *d. 1619*

Children

Elizabeth of Bohemia m. Frederick V of Bohemia *d. 1632* (✤ page 20)

Charles I of England, Scotland and Ireland *d. 1649* (✤ page 23)

The first Stuart king of England, James I, alienated his government and set the country on the path to civil war.

Louis' marriage to the daughter of Philip III of Spain cannot have been a happy one – the king seems to have made no secret of his homosexuality.

Louis XIII (1601–43)

KING OF FRANCE (1610–43)

House of Bourbon

Louis XIII came to throne at the age of eight. His domineering mother, Marie de Medici, ruled as regent until young Louis wrested power from her reluctant grasp when he reached the age of 15. For all Louis' desire to rule for himself, real power in France from 1624 lay in the hands of Cardinal Richelieu, whose religious beliefs clearly took second place to his political loyalties. In 1633 – in a move that garnered resentment from one side, pleasure from the other, and surprise from both – Richelieu brought Catholic France into the Thirty Years' War on the side of the Protestant German principalities and Sweden. It was a transparent attempt to reduce the power of Spain and Austria, and establish French dominance in Europe.

Louis had been married at the age of 14 to Anne of Austria, daughter of Philip III of Spain. The king flaunted a series of young male favourites at court and for 23 years the marriage remained childless. The sudden arrival of 'an heir and a spare' – Louis in 1638 and Philip two years later – raised questions about their legitimacy that remain unanswered to this day.

Royal Connections

Father-in-law: Philip III of Spain and Portugal *d. 1621* (⚜ page 14)

Married

Anne of Austria *d. 1666*

Children

Louis XIV of France *d. 1715* (⚜ page 28)

Gustav II Adolf (1594–1632)

KING OF SWEDEN (1611–32)

House of Vasa

Known as the 'Lion of the North', Gustav II Adolf was one of the greatest military leaders of the age. Blessed with a formidable intelligence and understanding of state affairs from a young age, on his accession he immediately set about transforming Sweden into a force to be reckoned with. The first years of his reign were taken up with resolving the wars he had inherited from his father, Charles IX, but with Denmark, Poland and Russia making peace, in 1630 Gustav turned his attention to Germany and the threat of the expanding Holy Roman Empire in the Thirty Years' War.

Loved by his soldiers as well as his citizens, Gustav was always at the forefront of the battle and was wounded several times. His military tactics and organisation set the standard of warfare for years to come, and even Napoleon I was said to have studied Gustav's methods. The great warrior king died as he had lived – leading his cavalry into battle at Lützen in 1632. He left the throne of a strong and unified state to his six-year-old daughter Christina.

Royal Connections

Cousin: Sigismund III of Poland *d. 1632* (✿ page 10)

Nephew: Charles X Gustav of Sweden *d. 1660* (✿ page 34)

Married

Maria Eleonora of Brandenburg *d. 1655*

Children

Christina of Sweden *d. 1689* (✿ page 25)

GVSTAVVS. ADOLFVS. M.R.S.

The direct royal line of the great Swedish king Gustav II Adolf died out with his childless daughter Christina.

Matthias (1557–1619)

HOLY ROMAN EMPEROR (1612–19),

KING OF HUNGARY (AS MATTHIAS II, 1608–18)

House of Habsburg

Matthias was already king of Hungary and Bohemia when he succeeded his brother Rudolf II as Holy Roman Emperor in 1612. He allowed his chief adviser Melchior Klesl, Bishop of Vienna, to pursue a policy of compromise between the Protestant and Catholic states. Unfortunately, rather than strengthening the empire as intended, this only served to antagonise both sides, particularly his devoutly Catholic brother Maximilian. Maximilian succeeded in ousting Matthias and placing Archduke Ferdinand on the thrones of Hungary and Bohemia by 1618, and it came as no surprise when the archduke succeeded as Ferdinand II on the death of the old emperor in 1619.

Royal Connections

Nephew: Philip III of Spain and Portugal

d. 1621 (⚜ page 14)

Married

Anna of Austria *d. 1618*

Children

None surviving

Matthias married his cousin, the daughter of his successor Ferdinand II.

Michael I (1596–1643)

TSAR OF RUSSIA (1613–45)

House of Romanov

From the late sixteenth century Russia had been embroiled in a period of political and social upheaval known as the Time of Troubles, which saw a series of pretenders trying to claim the Russian throne. This ostensibly ended when Michael Romanov was unanimously elected as tsar by the National Assembly in 1613.

His first actions were to sue for peace with Sweden and Poland. This latter truce allowed his father to return from exile, and he effectively ruled Russia on behalf of Michael until his death in 1633. For the rest of his reign, the kind and pious tsar remained led by his councillors. The dynasty he founded, however, endured until the twentieth century, and the end of the monarchy in Russia.

Royal Connections

Grandsons: Fyodor III of Russia *d. 1682*

(⚜ page 45),

Peter I of Russia *d. 1725* (⚜ page 46)

Married

1. Maria Vladimirovna Dolgorukova *d. 1625*
2. Eudoxia Streshneva *d. 1645*

Children

Alexis I of Russia *d. 1676* (⚜ page 30)

The election of Tsar Michael I to the Russian throne.

Ferdinand II (1578–1637)

HOLY ROMAN EMPEROR (1619–37),

KING OF HUNGARY (1618–25)

House of Habsburg

The oldest surviving son of Charles II, Archduke of Austria, Ferdinand was brought up a devout Catholic, and it was his religious and expansionist policies that instigated and gradually drew much of Europe into the Thirty Years' War.

He began his regime of Protestant suppression almost as soon as he inherited his father's territories in 1595, and it was not long before his eye turned to neighbouring kingdoms. Bohemia was then under the control of the tolerant Matthias, who was ousted in favour of Ferdinand in 1617. However, much of the Bohemian nobility was Protestant, and they staged a rebellion in an effort to replace Ferdinand with the Elector Palatine Frederick V. Ferdinand fought back successfully in one of the first actions of the Thirty Years' War. Not satisfied with his hereditary lands and the crowns of Bohemia and Hungary, Ferdinand next set his sights on the Holy Roman Empire. Backed by the Spanish Habsburgs, there was little anyone could do to prevent him taking the coveted title on the death of Matthias in 1619.

For the rest of his life, Ferdinand fought to retain his possessions and establish his own (and Catholic) supremacy in Europe. It was not as easy as he had hoped. The Lion of the North, Swedish king Gustav II Adolf, was a formidable opponent, and Ferdinand's hopes of success in the war were dashed when Catholic France unexpectedly ranged itself against the emperor. When Ferdinand died in 1637, he bequeathed his son an empire in chaos.

Royal Connections

Nephew: Philip IV of Spain and Portugal *d. 1665* (⚜ page 22)

Grandsons: Ferdinand IV of Hungary *d. 1654* (⚜ page 31),
Holy Roman Emperor Leopold I *d. 1705* (⚜ page 37)

Married

1. Maria Anna of Bavaria *d. 1616*

2. Eleonora of Mantua *d. 1655*

Children

Holy Roman Emperor Ferdinand III *d. 1657* (⚜ page 26)

Frederick V (1596–1632)

KING OF BOHEMIA (1619–20)

Nicknamed the Winter King, Elector Palatine Frederick V was the focus for the Bohemian Revolution against Holy Roman Emperor Ferdinand II. Frederick was a member of the Protestant Union that had been established to protect them from the long arm of the Catholic emperors. Married to Elizabeth Stuart, daughter of James I England and VI of Scotland, Frederick's involvement drew his father-in-law's country into the Thirty Years' War.

Holy Roman Emperor Ferdinand II, whose territorial ambitions led to the outbreak of the Thirty Years' War.

Philip IV (1605–65)

KING OF SPAIN (1621–65),

KING OF PORTUGAL (AS PHILIP III, 1621–40)

House of Habsburg

Philip IV is remembered as the man who presided over the Spanish decline of the mid-seventeenth century. However, his kingdoms were in a state of disarray when he inherited them. His father had left the running of the realm in the hands of untalented ministers and had ordered the debasement of the coinage to fund his lavish lifestyle. Philip IV was too much his father's son to reverse the country's fortunes. He allowed himself to be guided by the Count of Olivares, whose foreign policies were overambitious. He drew Spain into a protracted war with the Netherlands and continued its involvement in the Thirty Years' War.

Despite Olivares' efforts to banish the insecurity inherent in Spain's hold over Portugal, in 1640 Philip was ousted from the throne in favour of John IV. This was another nail in the monarchy's coffin, and three years later Olivares fell from grace. Philip continued to rely on new favourites and ignored the cries of his beleaguered people, believing that his resource-straining policies were serving God and his birthright.

Philip's reign saw the reinforcement and dissemination of the Habsburg bloodline across Europe. His first marriage, to the daughter of Henry IV of France, gave him seven children, the youngest of whom, Maria Theresa of Spain, married Philip's nephew Louis XIV of France. Philip's second marriage, to his own niece Mariana of Austria, daughter of Holy Roman Emperor Ferdinand III, yielded a further five offspring, including Philip's successor Charles II and Margaret of Spain. Margaret also married her first cousin, Holy Roman Emperor Leopold I.

Philip IV was a keen hunter and a patron of the arts.

Royal Connections

Uncle: Holy Roman Emperor Ferdinand II *d. 1637* (❦ page 20)

Nephew: Ferdinand IV of Hungary *d. 1654* (❦ page 31)

Married

1. Elisabeth of Bourbon *d. 1644*

2. Mariana of Austria *d. 1696*

Children

Maria Theresa of Spain m. Louis XIV of France *d. 1715* (❦ page 28)

Margaret of Spain m. Holy Roman Emperor Leopold I *d. 1705* (❦ page 37)

Charles II of Spain *d. 1700* (❦ page 40)

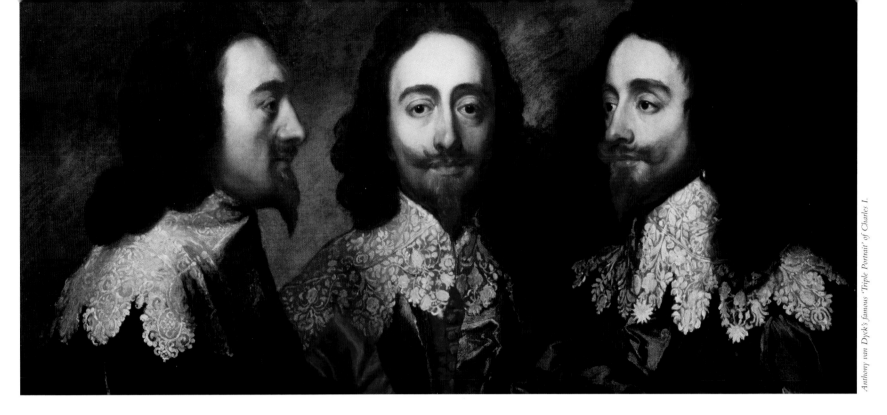

Charles I (1600–49)

KING OF ENGLAND, SCOTLAND AND IRELAND (1625–49)
House of Stuart

So deeply had his father's belief in the Divine Right of Kings been instilled into the young Charles I that he was unable to compromise with a parliament he considered treasonously recalcitrant. Parliament distrusted the king's chief advisor, the Duke of Buckingham, whose unsuccessful warmongering with Spain and France was draining the country's resources. The strict Puritan contingent among them also resented what they saw as Charles's 'catholicising' of the Church in England. In 1629, when parliament refused to grant him money, Charles dissolved it and ruled alone for the next 11 years.

When he was finally forced to recall parliament in 1640 its members laid before him a list of grievances, demanding extensive changes in his government. Incensed, the king attempted to arrest the leading members of parliament, but they had escaped the Commons before Charles stormed in. His action, however, set the stage for the Civil War.

Fortunes in the war vacillated between the Royalists and Parliamentarians, led by Oliver Cromwell. However, the king's method of playing off Scotland against his English foes backfired. When he was finally captured he had few powerful supporters. At his trial he refused to recognise the legality of the court and made no defence of his actions. He was executed in January 1649. His son, who had escaped to Holland, would have to watch his country being ruled by Cromwell for 11 years before restoring the monarchy in 1660.

Royal Connections

Brother-in-law: Louis XIII of France *d. 1610* (❧ page 16)

Cousin: Frederick III of Denmark and Norway *d. 1670* (❧ page 33)

Grandchildren: William III of England, Scotland and Ireland *d. 1702* (❧ page 52),

Mary II of England, Scotland and Ireland *d. 1694* (❧ page 51),

Anne of Great Britain and Ireland *d. 1714* (❧ page 62)

Married

Henrietta Maria of France *d. 1669*

Children

Charles II of England, Scotland and Ireland *d. 1685* (❧ page 38)

James II of England, Scotland and Ireland *d. 1701* (❧ page 49)

Right: Queen Christina of Sweden.

Left: Polish king Ladislas IV.

Ladislas IV (1595–1648)

KING OF POLAND (1632–48)

House of Vasa

Ladislas IV was the eldest son of Sigismund III by his first wife, Anne of Austria. Like his father, he continued without success to press his claim to the Swedish crown. He had also been elected tsar of Russia in 1610, during the Time of Troubles, but never ruled there either, the country instead coming under the leadership of the Romanov Michael I. Although Ladislas managed to avoid the devastation that might have been wrought had he joined the Thirty Years' War, his efforts at domestic reform were ultimately a failure. He died the year after his son, leaving the Polish–Lithuanian Commonwealth in the hands of his brother John II.

Royal Connections

Brother: John II of Poland *d. 1672* (❧ page 32)

Brother-in-law: Holy Roman Emperor Ferdinand III *d. 1567* (❧ page 26)

Married

Cecilia Renata of Austria *d. 1644*

Marie Louise Gonzaga *d. 1667*

Children

Sigmund Casimir

Christina (1626–89)

QUEEN OF SWEDEN (1632–54)

House of Vasa

The only child of Gustav II Adolf, Christina was six years old when she inherited her father's crown on his death at the Battle of Lützen. The first half of her reign was subject to the regency of Axel Oxenstierna, who ruled Sweden in Christina's minority. The queen herself was later subject to several marriage proposals by influential European princes, but she showed no inclination towards matrimony, and to prevent further advances she named her cousin Charles X Gustav her successor. Christina converted to Catholicism, and it is likely that her wish to openly practice her religion led to her abdication in 1654. She died in Rome.

Royal Connections

Cousin: Charles X Gustav of Sweden *d. 1660* (❧ page 34)

Married

Unmarried

Children

None

Royal Connections

Father-in-law: Philip III of Spain and Portugal *d. 1621* (⚜ page 14)

Married

1. Maria Anna of Spain *d. 1646*

2. Maria Leopoldine of Austria *d. 1649*

3. Eleonora of Mantua *d. 1686*

Children

Ferdinand IV of Hungary *d. 1654* (⚜ page 31)

Mariana of Austria m. Philip IV of Spain and Portugal *d. 1665* (⚜ page 22)

Holy Roman Emperor Leopold I *d. 1705* (⚜ page 37)

Ferdinand III (1608–57)

HOLY ROMAN EMPEROR (1637–57),

KING OF HUNGARY (1637–47)

House of Habsburg

When Ferdinand inherited the Holy Roman Empire, the Thirty Years' War had been raging for two decades, and the new emperor hoped to establish peace with France and Sweden fairly swiftly. Ferdinand had been created leader of the Empire's forces in 1630, but this was a nominal role, and it was General Gallus who led the imperial successes for the next few years. The disasters that followed Ferdinand's accession drove him to seek peace with his enemies. Despite this, he refused to accept peace at any cost and rejected early terms. Ferdinand took steps to ensure support during the negotiations to come including, in 1644, granting the rulers of all the German principalities permission to decide their own foreign policy. It was only in 1648 that the various protagonists – Sweden and France, Spain and the Holy Roman Empire, plus the Netherlands – finally agreed terms in the Peace of Westphalia.

From this time until the end of his life, Ferdinand focused on establishing administrative reforms that would help his lands and his people on the long road to recovery from years of war. For all his efforts, his reign marked the end of attempts to make the Holy Roman Empire a strong centralised state and the status of its monarch the most powerful in Europe.

John IV (1603–56)

KING OF PORTUGAL (1640–56)

House of Braganza

John IV oversaw Portuguese independence from Spain.

Descended from the sixteenth-century king Manuel I, John – then the Duke of Braganza – was the obvious focus for those wishing to restore Portugal's independence from Spanish rule. The Portuguese revolution took place successfully and in December 1640 John IV was voted king by the National Assembly. This began a lengthy war with Spain, but the diffident Philip IV had neither the skill nor the support to wrest back his lost kingdom. Despite this, the country did not officially recognise Portuguese independence for nearly 30 years.

John began securing his position against Spain by signing alliances with France and Sweden in 1641, but Portugal played only a small part in the Thirty Years' War. John had little interest in military affairs. He was a musical and artistic man, and during his lifetime he collected a fabulous library – one of the largest in the world at the time – most of which was lost during an earthquake in the eighteenth century. He patronised artists and musicians, and was a respected composer himself. John the Restorer died in 1656, the first king of an independent Portugal. The Braganza line continued in the successive rules of his two sons, Alfonso VI and Peter II.

Royal Connections

Grandson: John V of Portugal *d. 1750* (♣ page 65)

Married

Luisa de Guzman *d. 1666*

Children

Catherine of Braganza m. Charles II of England, Scotland and Ireland *d. 1685* (♣ page 38)

Alfonso VI of Portugal *d. 1683* (♣ page 35)

Peter II of Portugal *d. 1706* (♣ page 41)

Louis XIV (1638–1715)

KING OF FRANCE (1643–1715)
House of Bourbon

Louis XIII and Anne of Austria had been childless for 23 years when an heir was born to them. They named him Louis-Dieudonné – the God-given. Louis' mother, acting as regent, allowed herself to be guided by the influential Cardinal Mazarin. The years following were characterised by a series of civil wars known as the Fronde, in which French nobles and law courts rose up against Mazarin to preserve the ancient liberties of France by limiting the power of the king. The rebellion had been firmly crushed by 1653.

Louis was a believer in the Divine Right of Kings, and when Mazarin died in 1661 he announced he would take personal control of the government. France was already a leading power in Europe, and Louis spent the next 54 years establishing an administrative code of practice that reinforced and expanded this influence.

In 1660 Louis married Maria Theresa, daughter of Philip IV of Spain and his first cousin on his mother's side. Louis and Maria Theresa had only one child that lived to adulthood, Grand Dauphin Louis, but this was enough to not only secure the Bourbon line in France but also to see it established in Spain. A condition of the dowry had been that Maria Theresa relinquished all claim for her descendants to the Spanish throne. The impoverished Spain, however, never paid the dowry in full, rendering this condition void. France was drawn into the War of the Spanish Succession in 1701 to defend the right of Louis' grandson Philip, who had been bequeathed Spanish territories on the death of the last Spanish Habsburg, Charles II. A number of European countries, fearful of France's expansion, joined the war on the side of Louis' cousin Holy Roman Emperor Leopold I, who was staking his own claim to Spain. The war only ended the year before Louis' death. Louis was a cultured king. Under his patronage music, art and literature flourished in France, and palaces were built – including Versailles – on a scale of luxury never seen before. The Sun King died in 1715, four days short of his seventy-seventh birthday. His 72-year reign was the longest and arguably the most magnificent of any European monarch.

Royal Connections

Uncle: Philip IV of Spain and Portugal *d. 1665* (⚜ page 22)

Cousins: Charles II of Spain *d. 1700* (⚜ page 40),

Ferdinand IV of Hungary *d. 1654* (⚜ page 31),

Holy Roman Emperor Leopold I *d. 1705* (⚜ page 37),

Charles II of England, Scotland and Ireland *d. 1685* (⚜ page 38),

James II of England, Scotland and Ireland *d. 1701* (⚜ page 49)

Grandson: Philip V of Spain *d. 1746* (⚜ page 58)

Married

Maria Theresa of Spain *d. 1683*

Children

Louis, Dauphin of France *d. 1711*

Alexis I, the second Romanov tsar of Russia.

Alexis I (1629–76)

Tsar of Russia (1645–76)

House of Romanov

Alexis I was 16 when he inherited the Romanov throne from his father Michael I. His youth allowed him to be guided by Boris Morozov, once his teacher and now created head of the new government. Supported by the young tsar, Morozov set out a programme of domestic reform that envisaged a prosperous future for Russia. Most notably, a new code of laws was introduced, which benefited the landowners but reinforced the lowly position of the serfs, making it impossible to break free of their place in the class pyramid. The laws endorsed by Alexis were still in place in the early nineteenth century. He was also concerned with the Church and allowed Patriarch Nikon to instigate a number of reforms that resulted in a schism and ultimately the abolition of the Russian patriarchy.

Alexis wanted his country to benefit from western influences, and to that end he encouraged more trade with Europe than his predecessors. This resulted in an influx of western technology and ideas that allowed a modernisation of the army and navy. Such developments proved useful in the expansion of Russian territories, and it was during Alexis' reign that parts of the Ukraine were absorbed into the Russian empire.

Although not all Alexis' reforms were popular or successful, he laid the foundations for three of his sons to continue his work, culminating in the reign of Peter the Great.

Royal Connections

Daughter-in-law: Catherine I of Russia *d. 1727* (♣ page 72)

Married

1. Maria Miloslavskaya *d. 1669*

2. Nataliya Kyrillovna Naryshkina *d. 1694*

Children

Fyodor III of Russia *d. 1682* (♣ page 45)

Ivan V of Russia *d. 1696* (♣ page 46)

Peter I of Russia *d. 1725* (♣ page 46)

Ferdinand IV (1633–54)

KING OF HUNGARY (1647–54)

House of Habsburg

The eldest of the six children born to Holy Roman Emperor Ferdinand III by his first wife Maria Anna of Spain, Ferdinand IV was granted the crowns of Bohemia and Hungary as the Thirty Years' War drew to an end (in 1646 and 1647 respectively). This was part of his father's grooming to prepare Ferdinand to take over the reins of the empire, and in recognition of this he was crowned King of the Romans – future Holy Roman Emperor – in 1653. However, Ferdinand died the following year, leaving his younger brother Leopold as heir.

Royal Connections

Uncle: Philip IV of Spain and Portugal *d. 1665* (♣ page 22)

Brother: Holy Roman Emperor Leopold I

d. 1705 (♣ page 37)

Cousin: Louis XIV of France *d. 1715* (♣ page 28)

Married

Unmarried

Children

None

Ferdinand IV predeceased his father and so never became Holy Roman Emperor.

The decline in Poland's fortunes began in the reign of John II.

John II (1609–72)

KING OF POLAND (1648–68)

House of Vasa

John II was the son of Sigismund III by his second wife, Constance of Austria. He spent much of his life under the influence and control of his half-brother Ladislas IV, and after his election to the throne of the Polish–Lithuanian Commonwealth in 1648 he showed little aptitude for politics, either domestic or international.

The period of his reign is now known as the Deluge, an appellation that aptly reflects the troubles he faced. John inherited war with the Cossacks from his brother, and from this point it seemed that Poland was under attack from all sides. An early defeat of combined Cossack, Turkish and Tatar forces was not an indication of things to come. In 1654 Tsar Alexis I of Russia invaded Poland, the following year Charles X of Sweden swept into John's lands and there were rebellions in Transylvania in the south. With his resources scattered John put up a respectable fight, defeating the Transylvanian prince George II and at least managing to force a stalemate against the Swedish. By 1667, John had to cede large parts of the Ukraine to Russia, and although the Swedes retreated without gaining significant territory, Poland was in ruins.

John's marriage to his half-brother's widow remained childless, and efforts to nominate a successor caused resentment among the Polish nobility. Admitting defeat, John retired to a Jesuit abbey, where he died four years later.

Royal Connections

Brother: Ladislas IV of Poland *d. 1648* (❧ page 25)

Married

Marie Louise Gonzaga *d. 1667*

Children

None

Frederick III (1609–70)

KING OF DENMARK AND NORWAY (1648–70)

House of Oldenburg

F rederick III was not born to kingship. A younger son of Christian IV, he was groomed to oversee the administration of his father's German territories and the prospect of inheriting the throne of Denmark played little part in his education. His elder brother Christian died in 1647, and when his father expired the following year questions over the succession had still not been resolved. To secure the throne, Frederick was forced to accept a number of conditions imposed by the Danish nobility that severely limited monarchical influence. Despite these early concessions, Frederick later exerted his own authority and put an end to the aristocratic power that was contributing to Denmark's financial decline.

The dominating feature of Frederick's reign was the ongoing feud with Sweden. The fortunes of war at first swung in Sweden's favour and Frederick was forced to accept the Treaty of Roskilde, in which he ceded almost half his lands to his neighbour. However, the Danish king fought back and the Swedes were driven from Copenhagen in 1659, saving the country from ruin.

Royal Connections

Grandson: Frederick IV of Denmark and Norway *d. 1730* (⚜ page 55)

Married

Sophia Amelia of Brunswick-Lüneburg *d. 1685*

Children

Christian V of Denmark and Norway *d. 1699* (⚜ page 43)

George m. Anne of Great Britain and Ireland *d. 1714* (⚜ page 62)

Ulrika Eleonora m. Charles XI of Sweden *d. 1697* (⚜ page 39)

Frederick III set the wheels in motion for a constitution granting hereditary rights to an absolute monarch in Denmark.

Charles X Gustav, who was passed the throne by his cousin Queen Christina.

Royal Connections

Uncle: Gustav II Adolf of Sweden *d. 1632* (⚜ page 17)

Cousin: Christina of Sweden *d. 1689* (⚜ page 25)

Married

Hedwig Eleonora of Holstein-Gottorp *d. 1715*

Children

Charles XI of Sweden *d. 1697* (♣ page 39)

Charles X Gustav (1622–60)

KING OF SWEDEN (1654–60)
House of Palatinate-Sweibrücken

Charles X Gustav was the son of John Casimir, the Count Palatine of Sweibrücken-Kleeburg, and Catherine of Sweden, sister to Gustav II Adolf. Seeing a path to kingship through marriage to Sweden's heir Christina, Charles made overtures to his cousin. Christina, however, had no interest in him or anyone else. As time passed it became clear that her interest in ruling the country was also on the wane, and when she abdicated in 1654 she named Charles her successor.

He threw himself into the task of establishing a single unified northern state in Europe. His youth had trained him well for the job – heavily involved in the Thirty Years' War, he had become expert in both military and diplomatic arts, and was thus well-equipped to continue the task of expanding Sweden's territories. He declared war on Poland, claiming that it refused to acknowledge him as king, but was repelled from Polish lands. Charles regrouped and – undaunted by the coalition now ranged against him, which eventually included Poland, Russia and the Netherlands – he turned his attention to Denmark. He inflicted a humiliating defeat on the old enemy in the Treaty of Roskilde, a forced concession that in fact perpetuated the conflict for years to come.

As the 1650s came to a close, Charles began to seek peace with his foes, but he died while negotiations were ongoing, leaving the regency council for his five-year-old son Charles XI to conclude the peace.

Alfonso VI (1643–83)

KING OF PORTUGAL (1656–83)

House of Braganza

Alfonso VI, manipulated throughout his reign by first his mother and then his brother, Peter II.

Three years before his father's death in 1656, the 10-year-old Alfonso unexpectedly became heir apparent when his older brother – the talented and suitably kinglike Teodósio – died at the age of 19. A childhood illness had left Alfonso paralysed down one side of his body and mentally unstable. It was not an auspicious start for the burgeoning Braganza dynasty.

Alfonso was governed in his minority by his ambitious mother, Luisa de Guzman, and even when he attained his majority Luisa used her son's disabilities to continue exerting control. Although of Spanish birth, Luisa played a part in masterminding the wars between her native and adopted countries, and in 1668 she succeeded in wresting official recognition of Portugal's independence from Spain.

Luisa fell from the king's grace largely through the machinations of the Count of Castelo Melhor, who saw an opportunity for his own advancement in currying the malleable Alfonso's favour. Words whispered in the king's ear convinced him that his mother had her eye on the throne, and she was banished to a convent. In fact Alfonso should have guarded against his brother rather than his mother. Peter stole Alfonso's wife and gathered enough support to convince the king to hand over government of the country. He spent his last years ruler in name only, banished to the Azores.

Royal Connections

Brother: Peter II of Portugal *d. 1706* (✤ page 41)

Brother-in-law: Charles II of England, Scotland and Ireland *d. 1685* (✤ page 38)

Married

Marie Françoise of Savoy *d. 1683*

Children

None

Leopold I (1640–1705)

HOLY ROMAN EMPEROR (1658–1705),
KING OF HUNGARY (1654–1705)
House of Habsburg

The second son of Holy Roman Emperor Ferdinand III and his first wife Maria Anna of Spain (daughter of Philip III), Leopold was intended for the Church. In fact this was a career he would have much preferred to the trials of kingship, but when his older brother, Ferdinand IV of Hungary, died in 1654 he was thrust into the limelight as heir to the Empire.

Almost the entirety of his 47-year reign was spent locked in conflict on two fronts – the Ottoman Empire in the east, and France in the west. A Turkish invasion of Hungary was repelled but the agreed peace was relatively short-lived. When the Hungarians staged a revolt against Habsburg rule, the Turks backed the rebel leader Thokoly and war recommenced. In 1683 Vienna was besieged, but – with the help of King John III of Poland and the imperial general Charles V of Lorraine – this turned into a victory for Leopold. It was not until 1699, however, that the Turkish sultan signed a treaty acknowledging the sovereign rights of the Habsburgs in Hungary.

The biggest thorn in Leopold's side was his cousin Louis XIV. The Sun King's desire to bring Europe under French control had long caused concern among the other great European powers, and to protect themselves they had formed the League of Augsburg, a coalition committed to defending their lands against French invasion. Undaunted, Louis took advantage of Leopold's preoccupation with the Turks to invade the Palatinate in 1688, sparking the War of the Grand Alliance. French expansion was curbed by the Treaty of Ryswick in 1697, but four years later the emperor was forced to take up arms again as Louis and Leopold fought for the rights of their grandson and son respectively in the War of the Spanish Succession.

Leopold did not live to see its conclusion. He died in 1705, leaving an empire in turmoil successively to the two sons born out of his third marriage.

Royal Connections

Grandfather: Philip III of Spain and Portugal *d. 1621* (⚜ page 14)

Brother: Ferdinand IV of Hungary *d. 1654* (⚜ page 31)

Cousin: Louis XIV of France *d. 1715* (⚜ page 28)

Grandsons: Joseph I of Portugal *d. 1777* (⚜ page 88)

Married

1. Margaret Theresa of Spain *d. 1673*
2. Claudia Felicitas of Austria *d. 1676*
3. Eleonore-Magdalena of Pfalz-Neuburg *d. 1720*

Children

Holy Roman Emperor Joseph I *d. 1711* (⚜ page 64)

Holy Roman Emperor Charles VI *d. 1740* (⚜ page 66)

Maria Anna m. John V of Portugal *d. 1750* (⚜ page 65)

Charles II ascended the throne by right on the execution of his father in 1649, but did not rule until the restoration of 1660.

Charles II (1630–85)

KING OF ENGLAND, SCOTLAND AND IRELAND (1649–85)
House of Stuart

In the years of the Commonwealth, under Oliver Cromwell, Britain had become a hotbed of Puritanism and all activities considered frivolous had been banned. Charles, a lover of art, music and literature, reopened the theatres and encouraged a renaissance in the arts that earned him the sobriquet the 'Merry Monarch', and endeared him to his subjects despite his wayward habits.

Although married to King John IV of Portugal's daughter, Catherine of Braganza, Charles was a notorious womaniser. He entertained a succession of mistresses and unashamedly acknowledged his numerous children. The fact that he showed no sign of siring a legitimate heir was a point of concern to his ministers during his reign, and had implications long after his death. Anti-Catholic feeling was rife in the country, and many wanted to see the king's Catholic brother James excluded from the succession in favour of Charles's illegitimate son, the Duke of Monmouth. Charles resolutely refused, and died a Catholic himself, bequeathing his brother a divided kingdom and an unhappy future.

Royal Connections

Grandfathers: Henry IV of France *d. 1610* (⚜ page 12),

James I of England, Scotland and Ireland *d. 1625* (⚜ page 15)

Cousin: Louis XIV of France *d. 1715* (⚜ page 28)

Brother: James II of England, Scotland and Ireland *d. 1701* (⚜ page 49)

Married

Catherine of Braganza *d. 1705*

Children

James Scott, Duke of Monmouth (ilegitimate) *d. 1685* (⚜ page 49)

Charles XI (1655-97)

KING OF SWEDEN (1660–97)
House of Palatinate-Sweibrücken

Despite inauspicious beginnings, Charles XI proved himself a wise and careful ruler.

The marriage of the Swedish king to a princess of Denmark, Ulrika Eleonora, in 1660, might have been expected to ease the long-standing tension between the two kingdoms. Although the union was that rare thing in seventeenth-century Europe – a love-match – the countries could not be so easily reconciled politically, as the Scanian War proved.

Charles had not shown much early promise. He had come to the throne at the age of five and a reasonably competent council of regency had ruled until he reached his majority. What they had failed to do, it appears, was adequately educate the king in matters of statecraft, and on his accession proper he found himself facing issues of which he was largely ignorant. He made admirable attempts to rectify this and proved himself a worthy military leader in the Scanian War, concluding a peace in 1679 that left his territories largely untouched and finally drawing his country closer to Denmark.

With foreign affairs more or less under control, Charles faced the mammoth task of rehabilitating Sweden, introducing administrative reforms and slowly expanding the power of the monarchy by limiting that of the nobles. In 1682 the Riksdag granted him absolute power, and he is acknowledged to have used this wisely until his death in 1697.

Royal Connections
Father-in-law: Frederick III of Denmark *d. 1670* (❧ page 33)

Married
Ulrika Eleonora *d. 1693*

Children
Charles XII of Sweden *d. 1718* (❧ page 53)

Ulrika Eleonora of Sweden *d. 1741* (❧ page 71)

Charles II's reign witnessed a downturn in the country's strength as an international power, as well as its domestic glory.

Charles II (1661–1700)

KING OF SPAIN (1665–1700)
House of Habsburg

The reign of Charles II marked the decline and fall of Habsburg rule in Spain. Charles was the only legitimate surviving son of Philip IV, but it soon became apparent that the boy had physical and mental disabilities, and he was unlikely to have the strength of character required to carry the country to international renown. It has been suggested that his disabilities stemmed from centuries of Habsburg interbreeding, and there is good reason to believe this. His father had married his own niece, Mariana of Austria, and thus Charles's mother was also his cousin.

He ascended the throne as a child, and even after he came of age his mother acted as regent. Despite two marriages, Charles was unable to provide an heir. He therefore bequeathed his kingdom to Philip of Anjou, the younger grandson of Louis XIV and Charles's great-nephew. The action created an instant furore among other European leaders, each believing they had a greater claim to Spain. The War of the Spanish Succession only concluded in 1714, 14 years after the death of the last Spanish Habsburg.

Royal Connections

Cousins: Louis XIV of France *d. 1715* (❦ page 28),
Ferdinand IV of Hungary *d. 1654* (❦ page 31),
Holy Roman Emperor Leopold I *d. 1705* (❦ page 37)

Married

1. Marie Louis of Orléans *d. 1689*
2. Maria Anna of Neuburg *d. 1740*

Children

None

Peter II (1648-1706)

KING OF PORTUGAL (1683–1706)
House of Braganza

Peter effectively ruled Portugal as regent from 1667, when he seized power from his physically and mentally disabled brother Alfonso VI. The hapless Alfonso was exiled to the Azores for the rest of his life, and when he died in 1683 Peter was officially pronounced king.

Alfonso's marriage to Marie-Françoise of Savoy had been annulled less than a year after the wedding, based on claims that the king was impotent. In fact she had colluded with Peter in masterminding Alfonso's overthrow, and the two were married just months after the annulment. Marie gave birth to only one daughter – Isabella – and when she died in 1683 Peter took a second wife. Maria Sophia gave him six children, including the future John V.

The first years of Peter's reign were remarkably untroubled, but with the outbreak of the War of the Spanish Succession he was forced to take up arms. The Treaty of Methuen (1703) established a commercial and military alliance between Portugal and Britain, where Peter's sister Catherine of Braganza had been queen consort of Charles II. Portugal effectively became subservient to English whims with regards to foreign policy, and Peter found his country part of a planned invasion of Spain. He died in 1706, long before the conflict was resolved.

Peter II overthrew his brother to claim rulership of Portugal.

Royal Connections

Brother: Alfonso VI of Portugal *d. 1683* (♣ page 35)

Married

1. Marie-Françoise of Savoy *d. 1683*
2. Maria Sophia of Neuburg *d. 1699*

Children

John V of Portugal *d. 1750* (♣ page 65)

Michael I (1640–73)

KING OF POLAND (1669–73)

House of Wisniowiecki

Michael Wisniowiecki was the son of a famous military leader, and he seemed the ideal candidate for election as king of the Polish-Lithuanian Commonwealth when John II abdicated. He could not live up to his father's reputation in the battlefield, though, infamously losing a war against the Turks. He also struggled to cope with his country's internal politics and the in-fighting amongst the nobility. A member of the Order of the Golden Fleece, he had thereby pledged allegiance to the Habsburgs, and married the daughter of Holy Roman Emperor Ferdinand III. His short reign ended with his death in 1673, and John III was elected to succeed him.

Royal Connections

Father-in-law: Holy Roman Emperor Ferdinand III

d. 1657 (✠ page 26)

Married

Elenora Maria of Austria *d. 1697*

Children

None

Michael I of Poland allied himself with the Habsburgs through his marriage to Elenora of Austria.

Christian V (1646–99)

KING OF DENMARK AND NORWAY (1670–99)

House of Oldenburg

Christian V proved to be a popular king, and his people warmed to his humanity and dedication. He acknowledged his shortcomings as a statesman and placed his trust in his ministers, most notably Peter Griffenfeld. Through Griffenfeld the work Christian's father Frederick III had begun in establishing an absolute monarchy in the region was completed.

The ongoing conflict with Sweden dominated Christian's reign, in particular the Scanian War (1675–79). This attempt to reconquer the province of Scania in southern Scandinavia, which had been ceded to Sweden in the Treaty of Roskilde, was ultimately a failure for Denmark. Although Christian's navy gained supremacy at sea, the armies of the young Charles XI of Sweden proved intractable on land. The conflict was essentially settled when allies from both sides – France and Holland – agreed a truce, and Charles XI took Christian's sister Ulrika Eleonora as his wife. Unfortunately, the familial connection did not put an end to the long-term animosity that existed between the two countries.

Citing 'lovemaking' as one of his greatest pleasures, Christian proved it by fathering eight children by Charlotte Amelia of Hesse-Cassel – including the future Frederick IV – and six by his mistress, Amelia Moth, whom he openly flaunted at court, to the consternation of his wife.

Royal Connections

Nephew: Charles XII of Sweden *d. 1718* ( page 53)

Married

Charlotte Amelia of Hesse-Cassel *d. 1714*

Children

Frederick IV of Denmark and Norway *d. 1730* (page 55)

The young Christian V of Denmark and Norway.

John III (1629–96)

KING OF POLAND (1674–96)

House of Sobieski

When Michael I died 1673, Poland was struggling to hold its own amongst the great European powers and the onslaught of the Ottoman Turks. It seemed, therefore, that the election of John Sobieski as the new king of the Commonwealth was a prudent move. John came from a long-established noble family and had an impeccable record as a military leader – so much so that six years prior to his election he was created commander of the entire Polish army.

On his election he immediately set about planning the recovery of lands lost under his predecessors, and to this end he formed alliances with the powers of France and Sweden. He did an about-turn, however, during the Hungarian Revolution, when the Turks supported a rebel leader in attempting to overthrow Holy Roman Emperor Leopold I. Loyal to the Habsburg cause, John came to the rescue of the emperor, leading combined Polish and imperial forces to raise the Siege of Vienna, drive back the Turks and subdue the Hungarians. His luck changed later, and defeat by the Ottomans in a campaign over possession of Black Sea territories unfairly undermined his reputation and led to unrest among the nobles at home.

Royal Connections

Grandson: Holy Roman Emperor Charles VII *d. 1745* (⚜ page 84)

Married

Marie Casimir Louise *d. 1716*

Children

James Louis *d. 1737*

Fyodor III (1661–82)

TSAR OF RUSSIA (1676–82)

House of Romanov

In part due to ill-health, as well as his relative youth on ascending to the Russian throne, Fyodor relied heavily on his advisors for help in governing his realm. Despite his disabilities he was determined to improve the lot of his people, and he laid the foundations of reform that were so effectively built upon by his successor Peter I (the Great). He continued his father Alexis's introduction of western thought and culture, and presided over a number of military and domestic changes. He had two wives in his short life, but he fathered no offspring and Russia passed to the mutual rulership of his two brothers, Peter and Ivan.

Royal Connections

Brothers: Peter I of Russia *d. 1725* (⚜ page 46),
Ivan V of Russia *d. 1696* (⚜ page 46)

Married

1. Agatha Gruszewska
2. Martha Apraksina

Children

None

Peter I (1672–1725)

TSAR OF RUSSIA (1682–1725)

House of Romanov

The younger half-brother of Fyodor III, Peter was only 10 years old when the succession question reared its head. Like Fyodor, his brother Ivan had been born from Alexis I's first marriage and should therefore have been the automatic heir to the Russian throne. However, Ivan's disabilities raised questions about his suitability for the job. In the end the two were crowned joint rulers, although Ivan spent the rest of his life overpowered by his charismatic younger brother.

When Ivan died in 1696, Peter assumed sole rulership of Russia and set about reforming the country. He travelled throughout Europe, learning about western methods in order to help modernise his own country, and he employed many European industrial experts to assist him back in Russia. He insisted on western forms of dress and manner among his nobles and later among the populace at large, and enforced many other changes that were not always welcomed. However, his domestic reforms effectively set Russia on the path to modernity.

His foreign policy involved attempting an alliance against Russia's greatest threat, the Ottoman Empire. He failed to do so, and in the end agreed a peace with the Turks in 1700. His communications over this matter with other European rulers, however, sowed the seeds for a coalition with Denmark and Poland against the expansionist power of Sweden, and as the resulting Great Northern War proceeded, Peter defeated Charles XII, gained some limited territories and founded a new capital at St Petersburg.

Peter was a demanding, sometimes brutal man, not greatly loved by his peers or his people, but he undoubtedly earned his sobriquet 'the Great'. By the end of his reign, Russia had been transformed from a troubled, isolated country into an empire that could challenge the greatest in Europe.

Royal Connections

Brother: Fyodor III of Russia *d. 1682* (page 45)

Married

1. Eudoxia Lopukhina *d. 1731*
2. Catherine I of Russia *d. 1727* (page 72)

Children

Elizabeth of Russia *d. 1762* (page 83)

Ivan V (1666–96)

TSAR OF RUSSIA (1682–96)

Ivan was nominally the 'senior tsar' during his joint reign with his half-brother Peter, but his disabilities raised questions about his capacity for effective leadership and Ivan had little say in state affairs. None of his five daughters suffered the same disabilities, and one of them, Anna Ivanovna, later ruled as Empress of Russia for 10 years.

James II (1633–1701)

KING OF ENGLAND, SCOTLAND (AS JAMES VII)

AND IRELAND (1685–88)

House of Stuart

The arrival of the Catholic James II to the throne of Britain was not a welcome change for many. In fact James did not seek to destroy the Church of England – he simply wanted to reinstate equality for Catholics, who had long been sidelined. He was a man of little charm, however, and his questionable temperament made him few friends. He made too many changes, too quickly, installing Catholics wherever he could

and ruthlessly dismissing anyone who objected. His fate was truly sealed when his second wife gave birth to a son in 1688. In the ensuing uprising, an invitation was sent to William of Orange, the Protestant husband of James's daughter Mary, to accept the throne. James fled the country and was deposed.

Royal Connections

Grandfathers: Henry IV of France *d. 1610* (❧ page 12),

James I of England, Scotland and Ireland *d. 1625* (❧ page 15)

Cousin: Louis XIV of France *d. 1715* (❧ page 28)

Brother: Charles II of England, Scotland and Ireland *d. 1685* (❧ page 38)

Married

1. Anne Hyde *d. 1671*

2. Mary of Modena *d. 1718*

Children

Mary II of England, Scotland and Ireland *d. 1694* (❧ page 51)

Anne of Great Britain and Ireland *d. 1714* (❧ page 62)

James Scott, 1st Duke of Monmouth (1649–85)

CLAIMANT TO THE THRONE OF ENGLAND, SCOTLAND

AND IRELAND (1685)

The Duke of Monmouth was the son of Charles II and his mistress Lucy Walter. Although there were rumours that the two had married, making Monmouth a legitimate heir, Charles never confirmed this and refused to name Monmouth as his successor. He was executed after a failed rebellion in which he tried to overthrow James II and claim the throne.

Mary II came to the throne after her father James II was deposed.

Mary II (1662–94)

QUEEN OF ENGLAND, SCOTLAND AND IRELAND (1689–94)
House of Stuart

Mary was the eldest daughter of James II by his first wife, Anne Hyde. She felt little guilt at her father's overthrow – married to her Dutch cousin William of Orange, she was a follower of her adopted country's Calvinism and could not sympathise with James's Catholic beliefs. Her marriage was successful despite the lack of children, and Mary was happy to agree with her husband's stipulation that he should rule as king and not just consort. She bowed to him in all matters of government, but proved herself a capable ruler in her own right when he was away. She died of smallpox, leaving her devastated husband to rule a foreign country alone.

Royal Connections

Sister: Anne of Great Britain and Ireland *d. 1714* (⚜ page 62)

Married

William III of England, Scotland and Ireland *d. 1702* (⚜ page 52)

Children

None

William III (1650–1702)

KING OF ENGLAND, SCOTLAND AND IRELAND (1689–1702)

House of Orange

The arrangement by which William III came to the English throne was unusual in that although his wife was the real heir, he and Mary were invited to be joint monarchs. The Glorious Revolution, achieved without bloodshed, was greeted with celebration by the people of Britain, pleased to have a Protestant monarch once more. William was respected rather than loved by his subjects. He showed his mettle against James II when the latter invaded Ireland in 1689, bringing to an end the threat from the deposed king at the Battle of the Boyne the following year.

His greatest enemy was Louis XIV of France, who had supported James II's counter-revolution, and one of William's main aims throughout his reign was to limit French aggrandisement. To this end he formed a strong European coalition with Austria and the Netherlands, later joined by Spain. The War of the Grand Alliance ended in 1697, having succeeded in its aims of restraining the arrogant Louis.

William had been proactive in reconciling his wife with her younger sister Anne when the joint monarchs first came to England, and on his death the throne passed to her.

Royal Connections

Grandfather: Charles I of England, Scotland and Ireland *d. 1649* (❧ page 23)

Married

Mary II of England, Scotland and Ireland *d. 1694* (❧ page 51)

Children

None

Charles XII (1682–1718)

KING OF SWEDEN (1697–1718)

House of Palatinate-Sweibrücken

With a reputation for cold-heartedness and a love of being in the midst of battle, on paper Charles XII was the perfect candidate to succeed a kingdom with a long history of military and political strength. Unfortunately his enthusiasm for war was not matched by strategic experience and ultimately his failures cost Sweden its position as the most glorious realm in northern Europe.

Almost as soon as he ascended to the throne, he was faced with the daunting prospect of war with the combined forces of Peter I of Russia and his cousins Augustus II of Poland and Frederick IV of Denmark. In the Great Northern War that followed the young king lived up to expectations, scoring early victories against Russia and Denmark, invading Poland and deposing Augustus in favour of Stanislas I, who was more amenable to ending the Polish-Russian alliance. But at this point Charles made a fatal error. Forcing his depleted and weakened army to march on Russia itself, without his active leadership due to wounds sustained in the previous campaign, Sweden suffered a dramatic defeat. The king fled to Turkey, where he briefly enlisted the help of Sultan Ahmed III. The Turks proved to be turncoats, reaching an agreement with Russia the following year, and Charles was forcibly expelled from the country in 1713.

He made his way back to Sweden and immediately began planning an invasion of Norway. He died there in the trenches, leaving control of a much-weakened country to his sister Ulrika Eleonora.

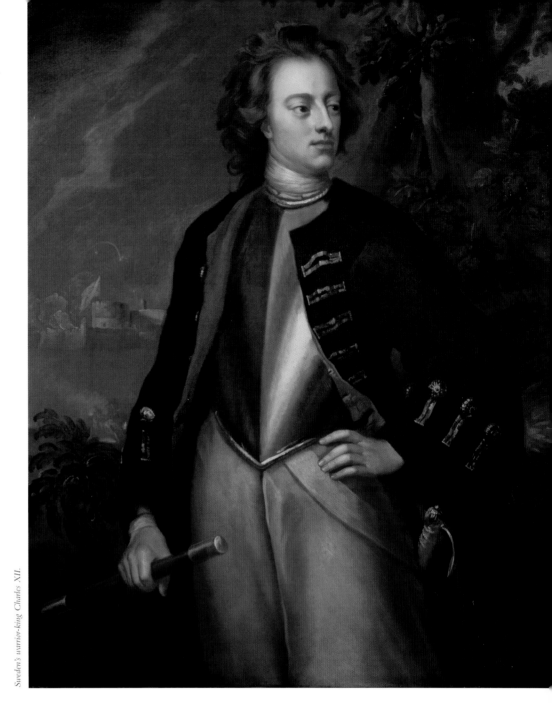

Sweden's warrior-king Charles XII.

Royal Connections

Sister: Ulrika Eleonora of Sweden *d. 1741* (⚜ page 71)

Cousins: Frederick IV of Denmark and Norway *d. 1730* (⚜ page 55),

Augustus II of Poland *d. 1733* (⚜ page 54)

Married

Unmarried

Children

None

Related to the royal houses of Denmark and Sweden, Augustus II was elected to the Polish throne in 1697.

Augustus II (1670–1733)

KING OF POLAND (1697–1704, 1709–33)

House of Wettin

Nicknamed 'The Strong', Augustus spent a large part of his youth fighting the French, and as he grew older the love of battle never left him. He became Elector of Saxony in 1694, in which role he played his part for the empire against the Ottomans, and when he succeeded in his campaign to be elected as king of Poland (for which he had to convert to Roman Catholicism), he continued his war against them – without resounding success.

In 1699 Augustus joined forces with Russia and his cousin in Denmark, Frederick IV, to carve up the empire of his other cousin Charles XII of Sweden. The Poles refused to be a practical party to this alliance and their king was forced to draw on his troops from Saxony instead. As a result he was roundly defeated and then deposed. Charles forced him to acknowledge Stanislas I as king of Poland. With the Swedish defeat at Poltava in 1709, however, Augustus felt the way was once more clear to claim back his throne, which he did with relative ease after renewing the alliance with Russia. Augustus spent the rest of his life trying to establish a hereditary monarchy in Poland. He failed in this, too, although his son Augustus III was elected to succeed him after a brief reinstatement of Stanislas. He was reputedly the father of some 300 illegitimate children.

Royal Connections

Grandfather: Frederick III of Denmark and Norway *d. 1670* (❧ page 33)

Cousins: Charles XII of Sweden *d. 1718* (❧ page 53),

Frederick IV of Denmark and Norway *d. 1730* (❧ page 55)

Married

Christiane Eberhardine of Brandenburg-Bayreuth *d. 1727*

Children

Augustus III of Poland *d. 1763* (❧ page 78)

Frederick IV (1671–1730)

KING OF DENMARK AND NORWAY (1699–1730)

House of Oldenburg

Frederick IV demonstrated many of the traits of his father, Christian V – both good and bad. He earned the respect of his subjects through a series of domestic reforms that included establishing several schools, reducing corruption among the aristocracy and taking steps towards recovery from national debt. He selected his councillors carefully and gave the impression of being accessible to the common people.

It was international affairs, however, that dominated his reign in the form of the Great Northern War. Here he formed alliances with Poland and Russia to continue Christian's campaign against Sweden, but in 1700 he was forced to agree to the Treaty of Travendal. Not willing to admit defeat, nine years later he reopened the war in an effort to win back parts of southern Sweden. Once again he failed against a strong foe, and in 1721 he conceded defeat.

Like his father, he courted scandal when it came to women, absconding with Anne Sophie Reventlow while still married to his first wife and mother of his two surviving children, Louise of Meckenburg-Güstrow. The Reventlow family took ruthless advantage of the situation to further their own ambitions, causing much dissent in the king's extended family even after his death.

Frederick IV's personal life was shrouded in scandal, culminating in his elopement with his mistress while he was still married.

Royal Connections

Cousin: Charles XII of Sweden *d. 1718* (❧ page 53)

Married

1. Louise of Mecklenburg-Güstrow *d. 1721*
2. Anne Sophie Reventlow *d. 1743*

Children

Christian VI of Denmark and Norway *d. 1746* (❧ page 77)

1700-1799

From the House of Stuart
to the House of Hanover

Anne to George III

Philip V (1683–1746)

KING OF SPAIN (1700–46)

House of Bourbon

The first Bourbon king of Spain, Philip V was bequeathed the throne by Charles II, the last of the Spanish Habsburgs, on his deathbed. His claim came through his grandmother, Maria Theresa of Spain, queen consort of Louis XIV of France and sister to Charles II. However, the fickle Charles had been expected to keep Spain under Habsburg control by nominating Holy Roman Emperor Leopold I's younger son Charles as his heir. Thus began the War of the Spanish Succession.

Although ostensibly a victory for the French, the war left the Spanish empire depleted both financially and territorially, and Philip spent much of his reign after 1714 attempting to recover these losses. His success on the battlefield was limited to reclaiming Naples and Sicily from Austria but he was more productive in his domestic reforms. Roads and canals were built, the armed forces were expanded and restructured, and the royal court itself began to take on a decidedly French character.

As well as securing the Bourbon line through the siring of five surviving sons from his two marriages, Philip began the process of reversing the decline in Spain's fortunes that had characterised the last years of Habsburg rule in the country.

Royal Connections

Grandfather: Louis XIV of France *d. 1715* (✣ page 28)

Nephew: Louis XV of France *d. 1774* (✣ page 70)

Married

1. Maria Louisa of Savoy *d. 1714*

2. Elizabeth Farnese of Parma *d. 1766*

Children

Louis I of Spain *d. 1724* (⚜ page 58)

Ferdinand VI of Spain *d. 1759* (⚜ page 86)

Charles III of Spain *d. 1788* (✣ page 90)

Mariana Victoria m. Joseph I of Portugal *d. 1777* (✣ page 88)

Louis I (1707–24)

KING OF SPAIN (1724)

For reasons best known to himself, Philip V briefly abdicated the throne in favour of his eldest son Louis in 1724. Louis never had the chance to prove himself as king, dying of smallpox seven months after his accession, after which his father returned to rule for another 22 years.

Philip V, over whose claim the War of the Spanish Succession was fought.

Frederick I (1657–1713)

KING IN PRUSSIA (1701–13)

House of Hohenzollern

Frederick inherited a strong and united province in Brandenburg from his father, the Great Elector Fredrick William, and it stood him in good stead when he later demanded to be recognised as king in Prussia, his other hereditary domain. Initially Holy Roman Emperor Leopold I was reluctant to acquiesce to such a request – in granting the title to one ruler he was opening the floodgates for every principality in Europe to establish a monarchy. However, when Frederick offered troops to support his cause in the War of the Spanish Succession, Leopold eventually agreed. He imposed the condition, however, that he would only acknowledge Frederick as king while he remained in East Prussia, which was not then part of the Holy Roman Empire. Thus, the first Hohenzollern monarch was designated King *in* Prussia, not *of* it.

It seemed that the entire continent was at war, but while Frederick kept his promise of imperial support to Leopold he managed to avoid the Great Northern War that was being played out between Sweden and Russia on the eastern boundaries of his lands. In truth, Frederick was little interested in battle, preferring pomp and display. He is remembered for the buildings he constructed and the lavish, intellectual court over which he presided.

Royal Connections

Cousin: William III of England, Scotland and Ireland *d. 1702* (♣ page 52)

Grandsons: Frederick II of Prussia *d. 1786* (♣ page 81),

Gustav III of Sweden *d. 1792* (♣ page 97),

Charles XIII of Sweden *d. 1818* (♣ page 123)

Married

1. Elizabeth Henrietta of Hesse-Kassel *d. 1683*
2. Sophia Charlotte of Hanover *d. 1705*
3. Sophia Louise of Mecklenburg *d. 1735*

Children

Frederick William I of Prussia *d. 1740* (♣ page 67)

Louisa Ulrika m. Adolf Frederick of Sweden *d. 1771* (♣ page 89)

Frederick William (1620–88)

ELECTOR OF BRANDENBURG (1640–88)

Frederick I's rise to kingship was in large part due to the success of his father in Brandenburg. Known as the Great Elector, Frederick William strengthened his own rule by limiting that of the aristocratic landlords and instigating a financial policy that allowed for the implementation of a large army. He bequeathed his son a principality already on the verge of great power.

The last Stuart monarch of Britain, Queen Anne.

Anne (1665–1714)

QUEEN OF GREAT BRITAIN AND IRELAND (1702–14)

House of Stuart

Anne was a kindly queen but lacking the intelligence to govern effectively on her own, and she left the intricacies of politics and administration to her ministers. Her husband, Prince George of Denmark, was of a similar temperament and intellect, and played little part in the running of his wife's realm. The greatest event in Anne's reign, apart from the War of the Spanish Succession, which lasted for a large part of it, was the Act of Union in 1707. This finally joined England and Scotland politically as the United Kingdom.

One of Anne's greatest sorrows was that despite 18 pregnancies, none of her children survived infancy. This was also, of course, a threat to the fragile peace of the kingdom. The spectre of the Jacobites – who sought to reinstate first James II himself, and then his descendants through his son from his second marriage, James Stuart – was ever present. To prevent a Jacobite insurrection if she died without an heir, the right of succession was settled on the Electress of Hanover, a Protestant granddaughter of James I.

The last Stuart monarch passed away in 1714 (reputedly buried in a square coffin to accommodate her large frame) and the throne of a united realm passed to a new royal house – with a ruler who could not even speak English.

Royal Connections

Father-in-law: Frederick III of Denmark and Norway *d. 1670* (♣ page 33)

Sister: Mary II of England, Scotland and Ireland *d. 1694* (♣ page 53)

Married

George of Denmark *d. 1708*

Children

None surviving

Stanislas I (1677–1766)

KING OF POLAND (1704–36)

House of Leszczynski

Chosen by Charles XII to replace the deposed Augustus II, Stanislas was little more than a puppet for the Swedish king, and had been elected as much for his weakness of character and willingness to be led than for any political skills or genuine affiliation he might have possessed. His first move was to pledge the support of the Polish-Lithuanian Commonwealth to Sweden against Poland's former ally Russia, and with the new king's backing Charles marched off to face the foe. The campaign ended in disaster and the Swedish king went into hiding. Without his support Stanislas was swiftly deposed by a triumphant Augustus.

When Augustus died in 1733, Stanislas' claim for reinstatement was backed by the French Louis XV, now his son-in-law, and this alone secured his election. The respite was brief. Russia would not tolerate a Polish king allied to France and put up an army to back Augustus's son. Eventually Stanislas admitted defeat and abdicated the throne in 1736. He spent his last years as Duke of Lorraine, which passed to France when he died.

Royal Connections

Great-grandsons: Louis XVI of France *d. 1793* (❀ page 99),

Charles X of France *d. 1836* (❀ page 125),

Louis XVIII of France *d. 1824* (❀ page 121)

Married

Katarzyna Opalinska *d. 1747*

Children

Maria Leszczynska m. Louis XV of France *d. 1774* (❀ page 70)

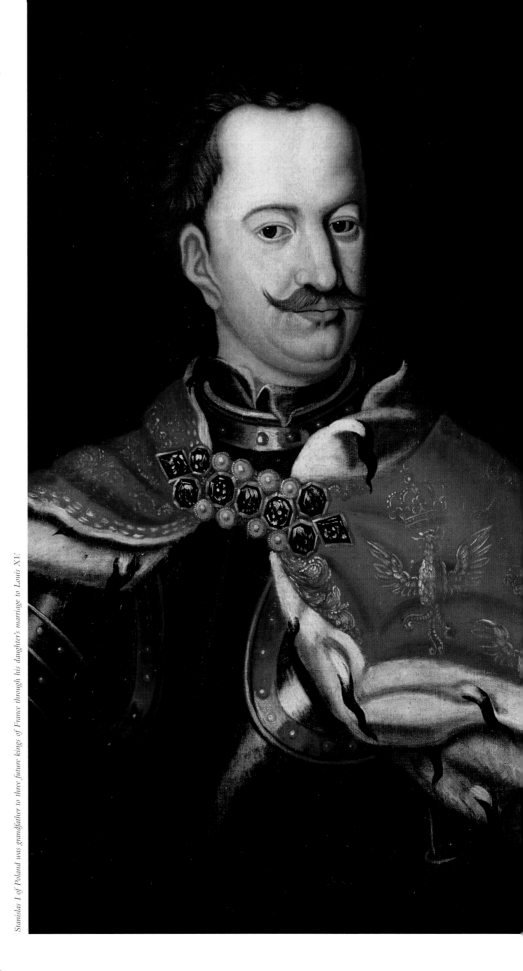

Stanislas I of Poland was grandfather to three future kings of France through his daughter's marriage to Louis XV.

Joseph I, ruler of Hungary and the Holy Roman Empire.

Joseph I (1678–1711)

HOLY ROMAN EMPEROR (1705–11),

KING OF HUNGARY (1687–1711)

House of Habsburg

Joseph was the son of long-serving Holy Roman Emperor Leopold I, and succeeded his father at the height of the War of the Spanish Succession. He continued to support his brother's claim to the Spanish throne against the French Philip of Anjou, grandson of Louis XIV. He did not live to see defeat in this campaign, and Charles VI had to settle for inheriting Joseph's empire. Had he lived longer Joseph might have proved himself as strong a leader as his father, but smallpox claimed his life at the age of 32.

Royal Connections

Brother: Holy Roman Emperor Charles VI *d. 1740* (⚜ page 66)

Niece: Holy Roman Empress Maria Theresa *d. 1780* (⚜ page 80)

Married

Wilhelmina Amalia of Brunswick *d. 1742*

Children

Maria Josepha m. Augustus III of Poland *d. 1763* (⚜ page 78)

Maria Amalia m. Holy Roman Emperor Charles VII *d. 1745* (⚜ page 84)

John V (1689–1750)

KING OF PORTUGAL (1706–50)

House of Braganza

Although only 17 when he came to the throne, John V had been brought up understanding the complex alliances that characterised Europe at the time. Three years previously his father had signed the Treaty of Methuen, thus involving Portugal in the War of the Spanish Succession. Although the Portuguese saw little action, John recognised the benefits of retaining the alliance with England once the war was over. He also married his cousin Maria Anna, daughter of Holy Roman Emperor Leopold I, strengthening his ties with Austria.

Despite this, his preference was for intellectual and artistic pursuits rather than the heat of battle. Wealth drawn from the newly discovered gold and diamond mines in Brazil – a Portuguese dominion – allowed John to indulge his love of architecture and to become a patron of the arts. He admired the lavish traditions of the French court and to some extent styled himself on Louis XIV.

John did not only use his wealth for personal pleasure, channelling much of it into Portugal's depleted economy and using it to raise the country's status as a European power. John's character is epitomised in the name he was given, 'The Magnanimous', and during his reign Portugal finally achieved the prosperity it had been seeking since it had wrested independence from Spain nearly 100 years previously.

John's reign coincided with a rise in prosperity for Portugal.

Royal Connections

Cousins: Holy Roman Emperor Joseph I *d. 1711* (❦ page 64),
Holy Roman Emperor Charles VI *d. 1740* (❦ page 66)

Married

Maria Anna of Austria *d. 1754*

Children

Barbara m. Ferdinand VI of Spain *d. 1759* (❦ page 86)

Joseph I of Portugal *d. 1777* (❦ page 88)

Charles VI (1685–1740)

HOLY ROMAN EMPEROR (1711–40),

KING OF HUNGARY (AS CHARLES III, 1712–40)

House of Habsburg

As the Spanish king Charles II lay on his deathbed he changed the bequest of his kingdom from Charles, younger son of Holy Roman Emperor Leopold I, to Philip of Anjou, grandson of Louis XIV of France. This sparked immediate war. When Leopold died in 1705 the Habsburg cause was continued by his eldest son Joseph, who encouraged his brother's claim to Spain.

In a way Charles's fate was sealed when he succeeded his brother as Holy Roman Emperor. Fearing the power inherent in a unified Holy Roman Empire with Spain, England backed out of their deal and instead signed the Treaty of Utrecht in support of France. By 1714 Charles felt compelled to sue for peace, and the Bourbon Philip kept his Spanish lands.

Charles's only surviving children were his daughters Maria Theresa and Maria Anna. To ensure the succession of his own line, the emperor introduced the Pragmatic Sanction, which stipulated that the crown could be inherited by women. The Treaty of Vienna endorsed this, but could not prevent the outbreak of the War of the Austrian Succession on his death, initiated by the new king of Prussia and leading to the election of his niece's husband as Emperor Charles VII.

Royal Connections

Brother: Holy Roman Emperor Joseph I *d. 1711* (❧ page 64)

Married

Elisabeth Brunswick-Wolfenbüttel *d. 1750*

Children

Holy Roman Empress Maria Theresa *d. 1780* (❧ page 80) m.
Holy Roman Emperor Francis I *d. 1768* (❧ page 85)

Frederick William I (1688–1740)

KING OF PRUSSIA (1713–40)

House of Hohenzollern

The son of the first king in Prussia, Frederick I, Frederick William learned the military arts fighting in the War of the Spanish Succession. His experiences at this time made him realise that Prussia's lack of military and financial resources forced it to be subject to the whims of stronger rulers, and he determined to resolve this problem.

Known as the 'sergeant-king', he believed the key to influence lay in military strength, and over the course of his reign he built up an army that was the envy of Europe. To fund this he instigated numerous domestic reforms that vastly improved Prussia's economy. He was frugal in his spending but fair to his subjects, including himself in the taxes he imposed. So successful were his financial policies that on his death there was actually money in the Prussian coffers.

Frederick William's mother was sister to George I of Great Britain, and he married his cousin, George's daughter Sophia of Hanover, in 1682. The couple had 14 children, 10 of whom lived to adulthood. Frederick William was notoriously cold towards his eldest son and heir, preferring his younger son Augustus (whose own son eventually came to the throne as Frederick William II), but he did bequeath a strong, centralised state upon which Frederick II could build.

Frederick William I allied himself to the royal houses of Britain and Sweden.

Royal Connections

Uncle: George I of Great Britain and Ireland *d. 1727* (❦ page 69)

Married

Sophia Dorothea of Hanover *d. 1726*

Children

Frederick II of Prussia *d. 1786* (❦ page 81)

Louisa Ulrike m. Adolf Frederick of Sweden *d. 1771* (❦ page 89)

George I (1660–1727)

KING OF GREAT BRITAIN AND IRELAND (1714–27)

House of Hanover

George inherited the English throne by virtue of his mother, Sophia, Electress of Hanover, on whose line parliament had bestowed the succession. She died two months before Anne, and George came to England with little knowledge of the politics or language of his new realm, and even less desire to learn about it.

Naturally this attitude did not endear him to his subjects, already unhappy about the arrival of a foreigner to lord over them. He earned himself a slightly sinister reputation – he had left his wife behind in Hanover and was reputed to keep her under lock and key, denying access to her children. Rumours abounded about his mistresses, one of whom he was believed to have secretly married. He also made regular trips back to Hanover, leaving the governance of England in the hands of his ministers – notably Robert Walpole, who is now recognised to be the first prime minister of the country. Like his successors George had a difficult relationship with his eldest son. He relied on him to interpret during government meetings but otherwise expressed no more interest in him than he did in the country he had inherited. He died abroad – on his way to Hanover, where his heart always truly belonged.

Royal Connections

Grandson: Frederick II of Prussia *d. 1786* (✤ page 81)

Married

Sophia Dorothea of Celle *d. 1694*

Children

George II of Great Britain and Ireland *d. 1760* (✤ page 75)

Sophia Dorothea m. Frederick William I of Prussia *d. 1740* (✤ page 67)

The first Hanoverian king of Britain, George I.

Louis' rule set France on the road to revolution.

Louis XV (1710–74)

KING OF FRANCE (1715–74)
House of Bourbon

S o long was the reign of the Sun King, Louis XIV, that both his son and grandson predeceased him, leaving the kingdom in the hands of his five-year-old great-grandson Louis XV. He bequeathed the child an internationally powerful but domestically troubled realm, and the internal situation did not improve during the regency of Philip, Duke of Orléans. After Orléans' death Louis selected his tutor Cardinal Fleury as his chief advisor, and under his pacific guidance the kingdom flourished. When Fleury died, Louis did not appoint another chief minister, and instead grew heavily influenced by a number of favourites, including his mistress Madame de Pompadour.

The king's marriage to Marie Leszczynska, daughter of the Polish king Stanislas, committed him to involvement in the War of the Polish Succession, the first of many conflicts yielding diminishing returns. The most disastrous was the Seven Years' War, at the end of which he had to sign over large tracts of colonial territory, including the whole of Canada, to Britain. The accumulated financial problems resulting from these wars eventually led to the outbreak of the Revolution in the reign of his grandson and successor, Louis XVI.

Royal Connections

Father-in-law: Stanislas I of Poland *d. 1766* (⚜ page 63)

Cousin: Ferdinand VI of Spain *d. 1759* (⚜ page 86)

Married

Marie Leszczynska *d. 1768*

Children

Dauphin Louis *d. 1765*

Ulrika Eleonora (1688–1741)

QUEEN OF SWEDEN (1718–20)

House of Palatinate-Sweibrücken

When Charles XII died, his sister Ulrika Eleonora claimed the throne as his closest relative. She was permitted to rule only after agreeing to abandon absolute monarchy, and thus began a period in Swedish history known as the Age of Freedom, in which the country was governed more by parliament than the monarch.

Ulrika had already acted as regent while her brother was at war, but she was largely influenced by her ministers and in particular by her husband, Frederick I of Hesse. On her accession she unsuccessfully sought permission to have him rule as co-regent rather than consort, and in 1720 she abdicated in his favour.

Ulrika Eleonora and her husband, Frederick I.

Frederick I (1676–1751)

KING OF SWEDEN (1720–51)

House of Hesse

Despite the length of his reign, Frederick was an unambitious and ineffective ruler. In fact, one of the reasons the Swedish nobles allowed his election as king when his wife abdicated was because they believed he would be easily controlled by them. They were right. Constitutionally unable to make any serious decisions about the realm, Frederick lost interest in it and distracted himself with courtly pleasures. These included the public parading of his mistress Hedvig Taube, who gave him the children that Ulrika Eleonora could not. Hedvig was the first official mistress – in the manner of the French – in Swedish history.

Frederick I inherited his lands in Hesse 10 years after becoming king of Sweden.

Royal Connections

Brother: Charles XII of Sweden *d. 1718* (❧ page 53)

Cousin: Frederick IV of Denmark and Norway *d. 1730* (❧ page 55)

Married

Frederick I of Sweden *d. 1751* (❧ page 71)

Children

None

Royal Connections

Brother-in-law: Charles XII of Sweden *d. 1718* (❧ page 53)

Married

1. Louise Dorothy of Prussia *d. 1705*

2. Ulrika Eleonora of Sweden *d. 1741* (❧ page 71)

Children

None legitimate

Catherine I rose from the Lithuanian peasantry to become Empress of Russia.

Catherine I (1684–1727)

EMPRESS OF RUSSIA (1725–27)

House of Romanov

Catherine co-ruled with her husband Peter the Great from 1724 and on his death the following year she assumed control. Her rise to the throne from extremely humble peasant origins was the stuff of fairytales. Peter at first made her his mistress, but married her in 1712 after divorcing his first wife Eudoxia. She repaid him with utter devotion and seven children, only two of whom survived. She was succeeded by her step-grandson, but her daughter Elizabeth later ruled Russia.

Royal Connections

Grandson: Peter III of Russia *d. 1762* (❧ page 83)

Married

Peter I of Russia *d. 1725* (❧ page 46)

Children

Elizabeth of Russia *d. 1762* (❧ page 83)

Peter II (1715–30)

TSAR OF RUSSIA (1727–30)

House of Romanov

The last surviving male of the Romanov dynasty was isolated and ignored throughout his childhood. His grandfather, Peter the Great, showed no interest in him and he was offered only a rudimentary education. With the backing the Holy Roman Emperor Charles VI, he was proclaimed tsar on Catherine's death. He had little time to enjoy his new status, falling ill with smallpox and dying on the morning of his wedding day – 30 January 1730 – leaving the female line to take up the mantle of Romanov rule.

Royal Connections

Uncle: Holy Roman Emperor Charles VI *d. 1740* (❧ page 66)

Married

Catherine Dolgorukova

Children

None

Peter II died at the age of 15, having ruled for only three years.

George II (1683–1760)

KING OF GREAT BRITAIN AND IRELAND (1727–60)

House of Hanover

George II should have been in a much better position than his father when he ascended the throne: he at least spoke fluent English, and the realm was economically and politically stable. However, like his father – whom he hated – he remained German at heart and once remarked about England, 'The Devil take the whole island'.

During George II's reign Britain's military and economic strength grew and its position as a power to be reckoned with on the Continent improved, with successes in the Seven Years' War against a French alliance that included Austria, Sweden and Russia. Overseas expansion and trade sowed the seeds of an empire that flourished for the next 150 years.

Robert Walpole remained chief minister from the reign of George I and continued to oversee the government of the kingdom until 1742. George II had little love of Walpole, but his patient and intelligent wife Caroline recognised the importance of having an Englishman direct English policy, and encouraged her husband's tolerance. The couple had nine children, but George had not learned from his own father-son relationship and despised his eldest son Frederick. He showed little sorrow when his heir died in 1751, leaving the path to the throne clear for his grandson.

Royal Connections

Grandsons: Christian VII of Denmark *d. 1808* (❧ page 96),
George III of Great Britain and Ireland *d. 1820* (❧ page 91)

Married

Caroline of Ansbach *d. 1737*

Children

Frederick, Prince of Wales *d. 1751*

Louise m. Frederick V of Denmark and Norway *d. 1766* (❧ page 87)

George II was the last British monarch to lead his troops into battle, at Dettingen in 1743.

Charles Edward Stuart (1720–88)

CLAIMANT TO THE BRITISH THRONE (1745)

Bonnie Prince Charlie was the grandson of the deposed Stuart king James II. There had been rumblings of a Jacobite rebellion since 1688, but the greatest threat of a Stuart revolution came with the prince's brief and unsuccessful insurrection in Scotland in 1745. He was driven out and spent the rest of his life in France.

Anna Ivanovna, daughter of Ivan V.

Anna Ivanovna (1693–1740)

EMPRESS OF RUSSIA (1730–40)

House of Romanov

Anna was a widow when she became Empress of Russia. She never remarried, and her lack of offspring further destabilised the Romanov inheritance – the throne passing between various offshoots of the dynasty. Anna was popular among the lesser nobility but sought to limit Russian aristocratic power by distributing the higher positions among those of German descent. She allowed the country to be drawn into the War of the Polish Succession and was involved in the decision to place Augustus III on the Polish throne. On her death Russia passed to her great-nephew, Ivan VI.

Royal Connections

Father: Ivan V *d. 1696* (✤ page 46)

Married

Frederick William, Duke of Courland *d. 1711*

Children

None

Ivan VI (1740–64)

TSAR OF RUSSIA (1740–41)

Empress Anna adopted her great-nephew Ivan when he was just a few weeks old, intending to make him her successor. He was duly proclaimed when the old empress died in 1740, but just over a year later he was overthrown by Empress Elizabeth. He remained imprisoned on her instructions, and later those of Catherine the Great, until his murder during an attempt to set him free.

Christian VI (1699–1746)

KING OF DENMARK AND NORWAY (1730–46)

House of Oldenburg

The son of Frederick IV and his first wife, Louise of Mecklenburg-Güstrow, Christian was a deeply religious man. His belief in Pietism, the Lutheran exaggeration of the personal and emotional aspects of religion, should perhaps have made him warm-hearted, but he had a reputation for intolerance and authoritarianism. As his reign progressed he fell increasingly out of favour with the Danish people. His wife was no more popular than he, and together they presided over a court lacking in the vitality and extravagances that characterised those of other European princes.

Although largely disliked, Christian's attitude was born out of a genuine desire for the improvement of his kingdom. He was a shy man but not an untalented administrator. One positive effect of his religious adherence, perhaps, was his tendency to pursue peaceful foreign policy rather than involving his country in war. He also oversaw improvements in Denmark's trade relations and industry.

Royal Connections

Grandson: Christian VII of Denmark and Norway *d. 1808* (⚜ page 96)

Married

Sophia Magdalen of Brandenburg-Kulmbach *d. 1770*

Children

Frederick V of Denmark and Norway *d. 1766* (♣ page 87)

The pious but unpopular Christian VI.

Augustus III (1696–1763)

KING OF POLAND (1734–63)

House of Wettin

Augustus II fully intended his son to succeed him on the Polish throne, but Stanlislas I, who had been interim king when Augustus had been deposed, was briefly reinstated. Undeterred, the young Augustus sought support from Russia and the Holy Roman Empire, and successfully secured his election.

In fact, during the 30 years of his reign, Augustus spent no more than three in the country he had fought so determinedly to rule. Lazy (he was known as Augustus the Corpulent) and disinterested in politics, he preferred leave Poland's administration to his ministers, allowing him to pass his time in Saxony, of which he was elector. He only fled the duchy on the outbreak of the Seven Years' War in 1756, but returned when the war was over. It was in part his neglect of his country that left the way open for the powers of Russia, Prussia and Austria to divide up Commonwealth lands in the Partitions of Poland that began in 1772.

Augustus hoped that his own son, Frederick Christian, would continue Wettin rule in Poland, but while he succeeded him as Elector of Saxony the Polish throne passed to Stanislas Poniatowski on Augustus's death in 1763.

Royal Connections

Father-in-law: Holy Roman Emperor Joseph I *d. 1711* (♣ page 64)

Grandsons: Louis XVI of France *d. 1793* (♣ page 99),

Charles IV of Spain *d. 1808* (♣ page 102)

Married

Maria Josepha of Austria *d. 1757*

Children

Frederick Christian, Elector of Saxony *d. 1763*

Maria Amalia m. Charles III of Spain *d. 1788* (♣ page 90)

Augustus III numbered Louis XVI of France and Charles IV of Spain among his grandsons.

Maria Theresa (1717–80)

HOLY ROMAN EMPRESS (1740–80),

QUEEN OF HUNGARY (1740–80)

House of Habsburg

Maria Theresa was a formidable woman, who exerted great influence over her husband and children.

When Holy Roman Emperor Charles VI realised he would not produce a male heir, he formulated the Pragmatic Sanction, which allowed for the Habsburg hereditary lands to pass to his daughter Maria Theresa. Other European leaders paid lip service to the sanction but on his death the War of the Austrian Succession broke out.

A coalition led by Frederick II of Prussia challenged Maria Theresa's claim in favour of that of Charles of Bavaria, the husband of one of Joseph I's daughters. In 1742 Charles was elected emperor, but his tenure was brief and in 1745 Maria Theresa agreed to the naming of her husband, Francis I, as emperor while she became empress consort.

For the rest of her life – and despite her husband and sons successively ruling in name – real power lay in her hands and those of her trusted chancellor Kaunitz. She governed carefully, initiating financial, educational and commercial reforms, and sought to alleviate the burden of serfdom. Highly moral and occasionally obstinate, the empress was also kind-hearted with a genuine love for her people. She is remembered as one of the most accomplished and effective rulers of the Habsburg dynasty.

Royal Connections

Uncle: Holy Roman Emperor Joseph I *d. 1711* (page 64)

Grandsons: Louis XVII of France *d. 1795* (page 106),

Holy Roman Emperor Francis II *d. 1835* (page 104)

Married

Holy Roman Emperor Francis I *d. 1768* (page 85)

Children

Holy Roman Emperor Joseph II *d. 1790* (page 95)

Holy Roman Emperor Leopold II *d. 1792* (page 103)

Marie Antoinette m. Louis XVI of France *d. 1793* (page 99)

Frederick II (1712–86)

KING OF PRUSSIA (1740–86)
House of Hohenzollern

S ubject to the incessant bullying of his military-minded father, the young Frederick spent an unhappy childhood that culminated in an attempted escape and brief periods of imprisonment and exile. Although he seemed to show more of an inclination towards artistic and intellectual pursuits, Frederick lived up to his father's reputation as the 'sergeant-king' when he came to the throne in 1740, and earned himself the title Frederick the Great.

His participation in the War of the Austrian Succession gained Prussia significant territories in Silesia, and he built on this throughout his reign, adding lands from Poland during the first Partition in 1772. During the Seven Years' War he fought off an attempt by an alliance of Austria, France and Russia to destroy his kingdom. Frederick was always concerned thereafter to resist Habsburg ambitions, although he never needed to go to war again.

His marriage to Elisabeth Christine of Brunswick-Bevern was loveless and childless, so on his death the Prussian throne passed to his nephew Frederick William II.

Royal Connections

Grandfathers: Frederick I of Prussia *d. 1713* (❧ page 61),
George I of Great Britain and Ireland *d. 1727* (❧ page 69)
Nephew: Charles XIII of Sweden and Norway *d. 1818* (❧ page 119)

Married

Elisabeth Christine of Brunswick-Bevern *d. 1797*

Children

None

Frederick II was descended from George I of Britain through his mother, Sophia Dorothea of Hanover.

Empress Elizabeth built on Peter the Great's modernisation of Russia.

power. Elizabeth resented the growing influence of the German states, particularly Prussia, and thus backed Austria and France in the Seven Years' War (which ended the year following her death with a Prussian survival). Internally she supported the power of the nobility over the serfs, who found themselves once more crushed by lords gaining increasing influence in the empress's government.

Despite being the focus for the attentions of many European princes throughout her life Elizabeth never married, and when she died the throne passed to her nephew Peter.

Royal Connections

Nephew: Peter II of Russia *d. 1730* (❦ page 72)

Married

Unmarried

Children

None

Elizabeth (1709–62)

EMPRESS OF RUSSIA (1741–62)

House of Romanov

The daughter of Peter I, Elizabeth had watched as the Russian crown passed between members of her close family without ever coming to her. First her mother ruled as Catherine I, then her nephew Peter II, her cousin Empress Anna and finally her younger cousin Ivan VI. Believing her claim to be stronger than any other, Elizabeth herself led the coup that overthrew the hapless Ivan and finally placed her on the throne.

Knowing she lacked an aptitude for foreign affairs, Elizabeth allowed herself to be governed by her advisors in international policy. The period of her reign saw the rise in Russia's status as a European

Peter III (1728–62)

TSAR OF RUSSIA (1762)

Peter was an odd choice for Elizabeth to name as her successor, given his Prussian sympathies and her abhorrence for the German ways he admired so much. When he succeeded he withdrew from the Seven Years' War, paving the way for Frederick of Prussia's survival. The move was unpopular and may have been one of the reasons for his assassination less than six months later, rumoured to have been masterminded by his wife Catherine, who succeeded him.

The usurping emperor Charles VII.

Charles VII (1697–1745)

HOLY ROMAN EMPEROR (1742–45)

House of Wittelsbach

While Charles VI was still alive, the nephew-in-law of the late emperor Joseph I acknowledged the Pragmatic Sanction that allowed the succession of the female Habsburg line in the form of Maria Theresa. However, on Charles's death in 1740 he immediately challenged her claim, initiating the War of the Austrian Succession. Forming a coalition with Prussia, France, Spain and Saxony, he invaded Austria in 1741 and secured his election as emperor the following year.

Maria Theresa did not give the upstart time to enjoy his new status and her troops swept into Bavaria. With the help of Frederick II of Prussia the Austrians were eventually driven out, but it was clear that Charles's position was untenable and he had ostensibly lost control of the empire even before his death in 1745. Maria Theresa's husband Francis was elected to succeed him.

Royal Connections

Grandfather: John III of Poland *d. 1696* (❧ page 45)

Married

Maria Amalia of Austria *d. 1756*

Children

Maria Josepha m. Holy Roman Emperor Joseph II *d. 1790* (❧ page 95)

Francis I (1708–68)

HOLY ROMAN EMPEROR (1745–65)

House of Lorraine

Francis was related to the Habsburg dynasty through his grandmother, daughter of Holy Roman Emperor Ferdinand III, and Charles VI liked the idea of marriage between his own line and that of Lorraine, who had been staunch supporters of the Habsburg cause through the years. To this end he brought young Francis to his court in Vienna at the age of 15 and raised him with his daughter Maria Theresa on the understanding that they would one day be married. An affection grew between them that was unusual in betrothed royal couples. They had 16 children, including two future Holy Roman Emperors and the ill-fated Marie Antoinette.

When the interim emperor Charles VII died Francis was elected to the imperial throne. In fact he was more than happy to leave the government of the empire in his wife's capable hands. Like her, Francis was popular with the Austrian people and the 20 years of their co-rule were marked by prosperity and development. His son succeeded to the imperial throne on his death in 1765, although most real power remained in the hands of Maria Theresa until she died.

Royal Connections

Grandsons: Louis XVII of France *d. 1795* (🌸 page 106),
Holy Roman Emperor Francis II *d. 1835* (🌸 page 104)

Married

Holy Roman Empress Maria Theresa *d. 1780* (🌸 page 80)

Children

Holy Roman Emperor Joseph II *d. 1790* (🌸 page 95)
Holy Roman Emperor Leopold II *d. 1792* (🌸 page 103)
Marie Antoinette m. Louis XVI of France *d. 1793* (🌸 page 99)

Husband of Empress Maria Theresa, Francis I.

Ferdinand VI married the daughter of Portuguese king John V.

Ferdinand VI (1713–59)

KING OF SPAIN (1746–59)
House of Bourbon

The second son of Philip V had an unhappy childhood, neglected by his step-mother who saw him only as an impediment to the ambitions of her own children. He grew up shy and, like his father, prone to depression. His personality was reflected in his policy as king, which preferred peace to war, but he could not always maintain neutrality in the battles between France and Britain. He was devoted to his homely but kind wife Maria Barbara, daughter of the Portuguese king John V, and never recovered from her death in 1758, dying himself the following year.

Royal Connections

Cousin: Louis XV of France *d. 1774* (🌼 page 70)

Father-in-law: John V of Portugal *d. 1750* (🌼 page 65)

Married

Maria Barbara of Braganza *d. 1758*

Children

None

Frederick V (1723–66)

KING OF DENMARK AND NORWAY (1746–66)

House of Oldenburg

Like his father, Frederick V sought to retain Denmark's neutrality in the wars that raged in neighbouring territories. Under the guidance of his minister Johann Hartwig Bernstoff, he even managed to avoid being drawn into the Seven Years' War. Bernstoff was a hugely influential and capable man, one of several on whom Frederick wisely relied throughout the course of his reign.

Domestically, Frederick continued his father's subjection of the Danish peasantry to the whims of the aristocracy and the military, and limited their free movement. The rise in interest in agricultural affairs that was sweeping through Europe at the time was reflected in Denmark by the establishment of a commission to investigate ways of implementing improvements in the countryside.

Frederick's union with Louise, daughter of the English king George II, produced five surviving children, including a son and heir. When Louise died in 1751, Frederick married again, this time to the daughter of Ferdinand Albert II of Brunswick-Lüneberg. Seven more children would be expected to safely secure the Oldenburg inheritance, but within a century the male line was all but extinct.

Royal Connections

Father-in-law: George II of Great Britain and Ireland *d. 1760* (🍀 page 75)

Grandsons: Gustav IV Adolf of Sweden *d. 1837* (🍀 page 105),

Frederick VI of Denmark and Norway *d. 1839* (🍀 page 118)

Married

1. Louise of Great Britain *d. 1751*

2. Juliana Maria of Brunswick-Lüneburg *d. 1796*

Children

Sophia Magdalen m. Gustav III of Sweden *d. 1792* (🍀 page 97)

Christian VII of Denmark and Norway *d. 1808* (🍀 page 96)

Joseph I's grandfathers were Peter II of Portugal and Holy Roman Emperor Leopold I.

Joseph I (1714–77)

KING OF PORTUGAL (1750–77)

House of Braganza

Despite a 27-year reign, Joseph I had no interest in or aptitude for kingship. He was more than happy to pass responsibility to his minister the Marquis of Pombal, and it was Pombal who ruled Portugal during this time. He saw the means to his own wealth, power and status through making the country a serious contender on the European stage, and to this end he instigated social and economic reforms that were not always popular. He rebuilt Lisbon after the earthquake of 1755, and under him Portugal was the first Catholic kingdom to expel the Jesuits. Effectively ruling the country, Pombal grew to be detested and he fell dramatically from favour when Joseph died and the crown passed to the eldest of his four daughters, Maria.

Royal Connections

Father-in-law: Philip V of Spain *d. 1746* (❧ page 58)

Married

Mariane Victoria of Bourbon *d. 1781*

Children

Maria I of Portugal *d. 1816* (❧ page 100)

Adolf Frederick (1710–71)

KING OF SWEDEN (1751–71)

House of Holstein-Gottorp

Adolf Frederick had four surviving children, two of whom later became kings of Sweden.

Adolf Frederick was elected heir to the Swedish throne in 1743, during the reign of the ineffectual king Frederick I. Royal blood ran in his veins – he was descended from Gustav I – but he was really chosen, like his predecessor, because the Riksdag believed he would be easily manipulated. After his accession in 1751, however, he proved less tractable than Frederick had been, making several attempts to liberate himself from the party chaos that had riven the Riksdag and to assert his own power. He was assisted in his attempts by his imperious wife, Louisa Ulrika – sister of Frederick the Great of Prussia – and later by his eldest son and heir Gustav. They had little success and it is unlikely that Adolf Frederick would have known what to do had he managed to break the bonds that tied the king to the whims of the Riksdag. For all his lack of courage and conviction he is reputed to have been a kindly man towards his family and servants, and he was much mourned on his death.

Royal Connections

Brother-in-law: Frederick II of Prussia *d. 1786* (❧ page 81)

Married

Louisa Ulrika of Prussia *d. 1782*

Children

Gustav III of Sweden *d. 1792* (❧ page 97)

Charles XIII of Sweden *d. 1818* (❧ page 119)

Charles III was the eldest son of Philip V by his second marriage.

Royal Connections

Father-in-law: Augustus III of Poland *d. 1763* (♣ page 78)

Grandsons: Holy Roman Emperor Francis II *d. 1835* (⚜ page 104),

Ferdinand VII of Spain *d. 1833* (♣ page 116)

Married

Maria Amalia of Saxony *d. 1760*

Children

Maria Louisa m. Holy Roman Emperor Leopold II *d. 1792* (⚜ page 103)

Charles IV of Spain *d. 1819* (♣ page 102)

Charles III (1716–88)

KING OF SPAIN (1759–88)
House of Bourbon

Charles was the eldest son from Philip V's second marriage, to Elizabeth Farnese, and his mother secured him the throne of Naples in 1735 in the expectation that he would never rule in Spain. But the death of his childless half-brother Ferdinand VI finally gave him the opportunity to prove his worth, and despite some unwise alliances early in his reign, Charles is generally acknowledged as the greatest of the Spanish Bourbon kings.

At first he attempted to maintain neutrality in the Seven Years' War between France and Britain, but the Bourbon ties eventually resulted in the Family Compact, an alliance between the Spanish and French branches of the dynasty. The timing was bad and Charles took his share of the French defeat, losing the American colony of Florida to Britain (this blow was sweetened by the cession of French Louisiana to the Spanish king). He won back Florida during the American Revolution, in which he backed the winning rebels.

He married the daughter of the Polish king Augustus III but only seven of their 13 children survived childhood. Through his daughter Charles allied himself with the Habsburg emperor Leopold II and passed the Spanish inheritance to his son, who became Charles IV.

George III (1738-1820)
KING OF GREAT BRITAIN AND IRELAND (1760–1820)
House of Hanover

One of the longest-serving monarchs in British history, George III's reputation was tarnished by the loss of colonies during the American War of Independence and his periods of insanity (now known to have been caused by porphyria). However, he was the first Hanoverian king to be beloved by his British subjects and presided over a largely prosperous period.

During the early part of his reign George's commitment to the unsuccessful policies of ministers he liked led to parliamentary difficulties as well as problems in America and Ireland. But by the time war broke out with revolutionary France in 1793 he had established a solid working relationship with Pitt the Younger, and the life-and-death struggle against revolution brought him a popularity he had never enjoyed when younger. His marriage to the amiable Charlotte of Mecklenburg-Strelitz was a successful union that produced 16 children. His bouts of illness had given cause for concern for much of his reign and in 1811 an Act of Regency was passed in favour of his heir George, Prince of Wales, and he never actively ruled again.

Royal Connections

Cousin: Christian VII of Denmark and Norway *d. 1808* (✤ page 96)

Granddaughter: Victoria of Great Britain and Ireland *d. 1901* (✤ page 137)

Married

Charlotte of Mecklenburg-Strelitz *d. 1818*

Children

George IV of Great Britain and Ireland *d. 1830* (✤ page 124)

William IV of Great Britain and Ireland *d. 1837* (✤ page 128)

Despite his German roots, George III prided himself on his Britishness.

Catherine II (1729–96)

EMPEROR OF RUSSIA (1762–96)

House of Romanov

Catherine was born into a noble German family and she was touted as a wife for the future Peter III of Russia in an effort to strengthen the ties between Russia and Prussia. The match was doomed from the start. Peter – weak, indecisive and immature – could only irritate his clever and ambitious wife. Within months of his election Catherine had convinced her lover, Grigori Orlov, to stage a coup, overthrow Peter and proclaim Catherine as empress regnant. Peter was murdered shortly afterwards.

The new empress initially demonstrated an enlightened outlook, but dreams of reform were shattered by huge Cossack rebellions in the 1770s. After that, she blatantly favoured the nobility and the peasants felt their shackles tighten as Catherine reinforced the burdens of serfdom that she had initially thought of easing.

In foreign affairs she presided over one of the great eras of Russian expansion. By 1764 she had established herself as virtual protector of Poland by placing another former lover on the Polish throne, as Stanislas II. During the following Partitions of Poland between Russia, Prussia and Austria, Catherine won the lion's share.

She also successfully tamed the Ottomans through the Russo-Turkish Wars recurring throughout her reign. Catherine entertained a string of lovers, several of whom exerted a great influence in state affairs. She had one son by Peter III – Paul – whom she treated with suspicion and refused to allow any say in government matters. She also had an illegitimate son by Orlov, Alexis, who was equally poorly treated by his mother. His half-brother Paul rectified years of neglect by giving Alexis the title of count just days after their charming but ruthless mother had died.

Royal Connections

Cousins: Gustav III of Sweden *d. 1792* (❦ page 97),
Charles XIII of Sweden and Norway *d. 1818* (❦ page 119)
Grandsons: Alexander I of Russia *d. 1825* (❦ page 112),
Nicholas I of Russia *d. 1855* (❦ page 127)

Married

Peter III of Russia *d. 1762* (❦ page 83)

Children

Paul I of Russia *d. 1801* (❦ page 107)

Russian empress Catherine the Great.

The last king of Poland, Stanislas II.

Stanislas II (1732–98)

KING OF POLAND (1764–95)

House of Poniatowski

Stanislas was the last king of the Polish–Lithuanian Commonwealth, and by the end of his reign a once-glorious kingdom had been dismembered and shared out amongst the power-hungry rulers of Russia, Prussia and Austria.

Stanislas was elected to the throne largely through the manipulations of Catherine II (the Great) of Russia, once his lover, who hoped through him to gain almost complete control of the Commonwealth. In fact Stanislas made some attempt to rule in his own right, sharing his countrymen's outrage at the first Partition of 1772. But his neighbour was too powerful, and repeated attempts to assert Poland's independence were crushed and the Commonwealth was partitioned out of existence between 1793 and 1795.

Under difficult circumstances, Stanislas managed to introduce some reforms, most notably in education, where he founded the Commission of National Education and the School of Chivalry. He also encouraged the arts, collecting paintings and planning the establishment of a magnificent gallery – a project he did not live to complete.

Married

Elizabeth Szydlowska

Children

Stanislas Grabowski

Joseph II (1741–90)

HOLY ROMAN EMPEROR (1765–90),

KING OF HUNGARY (1780–90)

House of Habsburg-Lorraine

For the first 15 years of his reign Joseph's authority was limited by the presence of his domineering mother, Empress Maria Theresa. While he outwardly deferred to her decisions he proved restless and unpredictable, formulating an extensive reform programme that he intended to initiate as soon as he was free of her influence.

The old empress died in 1780 and almost immediately Joseph began dramatic changes to the structure and administration of the Habsburg lands. He abhorred the disparity between rich and poor, and his reforms were aimed at bringing a greater social equality to his people. He formally abolished serfdom, dissolved monasteries and founded many aid institutions, hospitals, orphanages and workhouses. He also worked towards limiting the hereditary power of nobles and the clergy.

Such extreme measures endeared him to the common people, who held him up as their champion and saviour, but they made him several enemies among the upper classes and many of his reforms did not survive him. His unyielding personality had brought many of his dominions into revolt by the time he died.

Royal Connections

Father-in-law: Holy Roman Emperor Charles VII *d.1745* (⚜ page 84)

Brother-in-law: Louis XVI of France *d. 1793* (⚜ page 99)

Married

1. Isabella Maria of Parma *d. 1763*

2. Maria Josepha of Bavaria *d. 1767*

Children

None

Joseph II was greatly admired by the common people, but resented by the nobility.

Christian VII was mentally unstable and unpopular among his ministers.

Christian VII (1749–1808)

KING OF DENMARK AND NORWAY (1766–1808)

House of Oldenburg

The reign of Christian VII had parallels with that of his cousin (and brother-in-law) George III of England. He suffered recurring bouts of mental illness that are now attributed to schizophrenia.

Despite his illness, Christian had much more personal charisma than either his father or grandfather, but he lacked the education to make it work in his favour. Johann Hartwig Bernstoff at first continued his ministerial role from Frederick V's reign, but as the king became ill he turned increasingly to his doctor, Struensee, for advice and counsel.

Christian married his English cousin Caroline, but famously proclaimed that he could never love her and embarked on a series of flagrant affairs that drove his wife into the arms of Struensee. It has been suggested that her daughter, Princess Louise, was not of the king's blood at all, but Struensee's. When the latter was overthrown and executed by opponents of his increasingly eccentric policies, Christian had his marriage annulled and his wife exiled to Celle, where she was permitted no contact with her children. By 1784, increasing periods of insanity forced Christian to cede power to his son Frederick VI.

Royal Connections

Cousin: George III of Great Britain and Ireland *d. 1820* (❧ page 91)

Married

Caroline Matilda of Wales *d. 1775*

Children

Frederick VI of Denmark *d. 1839* (❧ page 142)

Gustav III (1746-92)

KING OF SWEDEN (1771–92)

House of Holstein-Gottorp

A capable and progressive king, Gustav III took major steps towards re-establishing the monarchical power that had been lost to the Riksdag during the reigns of his predecessors. The country he inherited was torn between the two opposing political factions of the Hat party and the Cap party (the former in favour of French alliance, the latter Pro-Russian). Determined to break Swedish subservience to foreigners, the new king staged a coup that restored royal power. Freed of most parliamentary control, he set about making improvements that would benefit his people and revitalise Sweden's military reputation in Europe, but a war with Russia between 1788 and 1790 proved disastrous and the last two years of his reign were ones of constant political crisis.

His marriage to the king of Denmark's daughter Sophia Magdalena was not a happy one, although it provided him with an heir. He distracted himself with artistic and cultural pursuits in a coffer-draining attempt to emulate French courtly life, by which he was much impressed. Increasingly obsessed by the dangers posed by the French Revolution, but prepared to promote social antagonisms in Sweden in order to maintain his own power, he was assassinated by discontented noblemen.

An educated man, Gustav III was a competent playwright.

Royal Connections

Uncle: Frederick II of Prussia *d. 1786* (✤ page 81)

Father-in-law: Frederick V of Denmark and Norway *d. 1766* (✤ page 87)

Married

Sophia Magdalena of Denmark *d. 1813*

Children

Gustav IV Adolf of Sweden *d. 1837* (✤ page 105)

The ill-fated Louis XVI died on the guillotine during the French Revolution.

Louis XVI (1754-93)

KING OF FRANCE (1774–92)

House of Bourbon

Louis inherited the French crown on the death of his grandfather Louis XV. Indecisive and weak, Louis was ill-equipped to deal with the catastrophe that was about to be unleashed on France by the monarchy's inability to pay for its international ambitions after involvement in the American War of Independence.

Attempts to avoid bankruptcy led to the convocation of the Estates-General, whose members proclaimed themselves the National Assembly with sovereign power, thus inaugurating the French Revolution. Royal reluctance to accept this was only overcome when the people of Paris stormed the Bastille on 14 July 1789. Subsequently the royal family was forced to move from Versailles to Paris, from where they made an abortive escape attempt in 1791, leaving behind a denunciation of the work of the Revolution. This sealed their fate, the king was never trusted again, and on 10 August 1792 the monarchy was overthrown. Louis was put on trial for crimes against the nation, found guilty and sent to the guillotine in January 1793. His unpopular queen Marie Antoinette went to the scaffold in October of the same year, leaving their young son as nominal king.

Royal Connections

Father-in-law: Holy Roman Emperor Francis I *d. 1765* (⚜ page 85)

Cousin: Charles IV of Spain *d. 1819* (⚜ page 102)

Married

Marie Antoinette of Austria *d. 1793*

Children

Louis XVII of France *d. 1795* (⚜ page 106)

Maria's mother was the daughter of Philip V of Spain.

Maria I (1734–1816)

QUEEN OF PORTUGAL (1777–1816)

House of Braganza

The first thing Maria did on coming to the Portuguese thrown was to cast out her father's minister the Marquis de Pombal, who had been ruling with an iron fist for 27 years. It was a popular move. She had been married some years previously to her uncle, and he ruled with her as co-regent (as Peter III) but even with his support Maria soon found the pressures of government taking a toll on her health, both physically and mentally. By 1799, with her husband dead, Maria's son John was appointed regent and Maria effectively retired from government for the rest of her life.

Royal Connections

Grandfathers: Philip V of Spain *d. 1746* (❀ page 58),

John V of Portugal *d. 1750* (❀ page 65)

Married

Peter III of Portugal *d. 1786*

Children

John VI of Portugal *d. 1826* (❀ page 122)

Frederick William II (1744–97)

KING OF PRUSSIA (1786–97)
House of Hohenzollern

Frederick William inherited the Prussian throne from his uncle, Frederick the Great. Although lacking the natural leadership qualities of his predecessor, under him Prussia enjoyed further expansion, particularly through the Partitions of Poland. He initially supported the royalist cause in the French Revolution, but his invasion of France in 1792 was defeated and in any case he was more interested in dismembering Poland. He was also responsible for a flourishing of cultural activity at the Prussian court. He was a great music-lover and entertained Mozart and Beethoven, both of whom dedicated pieces to him.

Royal Connections

Grandson: Frederick William IV of Prussia *d. 1861* (❧ page 140)

Married

1. Elizabeth Christine of Brunswick *d. 1840*
2. Frederika Louisa of Hesse-Darmstadt *d. 1805*

Children

Frederick William III of Prussia *d. 1840* (❧ page 108)
Frederika Louisa Wilhelmina m.
William I of the Netherlands *d. 1843* (❧ page 120)

Frederick William II had eight children by his second wife, including Frederick William III.

Charles IV was forced to abdicate by Napoleon I.

Charles IV (1748–1819)

KING OF SPAIN (1788–1808)

House of Bourbon

Charles IV was the second son of Charles III and Maria Amalia of Saxony (daughter of the Polish king Augustus III), but even before his elder brother Philip died in 1777 the succession had fallen to Charles due to Philip's imbecility. As it transpired he was little more suited to the role of king.

By 1792 he had relinquished practically all responsibility for Spain to his chief minister Godoy. Under Godoy's direction, Spain found itself pitted against France in the revolutionary wars but, fearing himself on the losing side, he made peace in 1795. He went one step further the following year by forming an active alliance with his former enemy against Great Britain. After a series of humiliating defeats, Godoy was overthrown and by 1808, Charles's own people turned against him and he was forced to abdicate in favour of his son Ferdinand. Such a turn of events played right into the hands of the marauding Napoleon who, through devious means, shortly secured the abdication of both father and son, and placed his brother Joseph I on the throne of Spain.

Royal Connections

Grandfathers: Philip V of Spain *d. 1746* (✤ page 58),
Augustus III of Poland *d. 1763* (✤ page 78)
Cousins: Louis XVI of France *d. 1793* (✤ page 99),
Holy Roman Emperor Francis II *d. 1835* (✤ page 104)

Married

Maria Louisa of Parma *d. 1819*

Children

Charlotte Joachina Teresa m. John VI of Portugal *d. 1826* (✤ page 122)
Ferdinand VII of Spain *d. 1833* (✤ page 116)

Leopold II (1747–92)

House of Habsburg-Lorraine

The programme of widespread reforms Leopold's brother had initiated might have improved the lot of the peasantry, but it had earned the ridicule and resentment of the Austrian nobility at a time when the French Revolution seemed to be threatening the whole of Europe. Leopold immediately began retracting many of Joseph's policies. Like the other European rulers, the emperor was disinclined to get involved in French affairs, but saw little option. His sister, Marie Antoinette, was married to Louis XVI of France and was appealing to her brother for support. In 1791 he issued the Declaration of Pillnitz with the Prussian king Frederick William II, stating that that if other European powers would join them, they were ready to take a stand against the French rebels and restore the king's power by force. It was an empty threat, and Leopold knew it. Both Britain and Russia had made it clear they would not act, and the emperor hoped in this way to assuage his conscience and simultaneously avoid intervention. The Declaration began a drift towards war, but Leopold did not live to see it, dying suddenly after only two years of rule.

Leopold II's sister, Marie Antoinette was married to Louis XVI of France.

Royal Connections

Father-in-law: Charles III of Spain *d. 1788* (♣ page 90)

Brother: Holy Roman Emperor Joseph II *d. 1790* (♣ page 95)

Nephew: Louis XVII of France *d. 1795* (♣ page 106)

Married

Maria Louisa of Spain *d. 1792*

Children

Holy Roman Emperor Francis II *d. 1835* (♣ page 104)

Although allied through his daughter's marriage, Francis II was instrumental in Napoleon's downfall.

Francis II (1768–1835)

HOLY ROMAN EMPEROR (1792–1806),

EMPEROR OF AUSTRIA (AS FRANCIS I, 1804–35),

KING OF HUNGARY (1792–1835)

House of Habsburg-Lorraine

Within 14 years of succeeding his father as Holy Roman Emperor, Francis had presided over the dissolution of the oldest political organisation in Europe. The empire was broken up and the authority of the Habsburgs – that most ubiquitous of royal families – confined to their hereditary dominions of Austria, Hungary and Bohemia.

The revolutionary wars broke out just weeks after Francis's accession and later he was forced to stand against the might of Napoleon. Defeated in 1797 and again in 1801 he had to recognise that the Holy Roman Empire could not survive. It was formally dissolved five years later, after the Austrian defeat in the Battle of Austerlitz. Nevertheless, in 1809 Francis declared war once again, thinking that Napoleon's Spanish campaign might have weakened his strength and distracted his attention. He was wrong, another defeat followed, and the Austrian domains were only saved from complete dismemberment by Francis's agreement to the marriage of his daughter Marie Louise to the French emperor.

In 1813 he rallied once more, joining forces with Russia, Prussia and Britain in their last stand against his son-in-law, and here he finally exonerated himself. Austria's role in the ultimate defeat of Napoleon was significant, and Francis oversaw the Congress of Vienna that planned the restructuring of continental Europe in the aftermath of war.

Royal Connections

Cousins: Ferdinand VII of Spain *d. 1833* (⚜ page 116),

Louis XVII of France *d. 1795* (⚜ page 106)

Married

1. Elisabeth of Württemberg *d. 1790*

2. Maria Teresa of the Two Sicilies *d. 1807*

3. Maria Ludovike of Austria-Este *d. 1816*

4. Caroline Augusta of Bavaria *d. 1873*

Children

Marie Louise m. Napoleon I of France *d. 1821* (⚜ page 115)

Ferdinand I of Austria *d. 1875* (⚜ page 135)

Gustav IV Adolf (1778–1837)

KING OF SWEDEN (1792–1809)

House of Holstein-Gottorp

Gustav IV Adolf was 14 when his father was assassinated, and his uncle Charles (later Charles XIII) acted as regent until the young king attained his majority in 1796. As soon as this happened, he demonstrated his despotic nature by dismissing any minister who might still be under his uncle's influence. He continued his father's policy by taking a disastrous stand against Napoleon. The 1805 campaign of the Third Coalition against France failed miserably, and left his forces desperately weakened. When Russia turned on him, the king found himself alone and unpopular. As the Russians advanced and the king seemed powerless to resist, a group of army officers staged a coup and his uncle was offered leadership of a provisional government. The royal family were sent into exile in Switzerland.

Gustav Adolf had three daughters and two sons by his wife Frederica of Baden, but the crown prince, Gustav, was destined never to be king. Supporters of the deposed monarch tried without fail get the prince recognised as Gustav Adolf's successor, but he had to settle for the title Prince of Vasa and know that he and his descendants were forever barred from the Swedish succession.

Royal Connections

Grandfather: Frederick V of Denmark and Norway *d. 1766* (♣ page 87)

Married

Frederica Dorothea Wilhelmina of Baden *d. 1826*

Children

Gustav, Prince of Vasa *d. 1877*

Gustav was only 14 when he became king

The young son of Louis XVI and Marie Antoinette, Louis XVII.

Louis XVII (1785–95)

KING OF FRANCE (1793–95)

House of Bourbon

The son of Louis XVI and Marie Antoinette was king in name only for two years of his short life. Members of the French royal family who had fled the country to escape the Revolution proclaimed him to be the rightful king after his father was sent to the guillotine, but young Louis was kept captive the entire time in Paris, and he died in prison at the age of 10. Many believed that the boy had been the subject of a rescue plot and had in fact survived, but DNA tests in 2000 proved that this was not the case.

Royal Connections

Uncles: Holy Roman Emperor Joseph II *d. 1790* (⚜ page 95),
Holy Roman Emperor Leopold II *d. 1792* (⚜ page 103)

Married

Unmarried

Children

None

Paul I (1754–1801)

Tsar of Russia (1796–1801)

House of Romanov

Paul I was assassinated after five years of rule.

Although the only legitimate son of Catherine the Great the two had never been close, and as Paul grew older he strongly opposed several of her policies, particularly her favouring of the nobility and her expansionist plans. As a result Catherine kept him a virtual prisoner and attempted to change the succession in favour of his son Alexander.

When his mother died Paul immediately began working towards reducing the powers of the nobility and improving the lot of the serfs. He oversaw several developments in the military and economy. Always unbalanced, he extended his reforms to encompass personal whims such as banning travel abroad and introducing a form of dress code. The nobility, already resentful of the reduction in their influence, felt Paul was growing too despotic and arranged his murder in 1801.

Royal Connections

Grandsons: William III of the Netherlands *d. 1890* (❧ page 144),

Alexander II of Russia *d. 1881* (❧ page 147)

Married

Sophie Dorothea of Württemberg *d. 1801*

Children

Alexander I of Russia *d. 1825* (❧ page 112)

Nicholas I of Russia *d. 1855* (❧ page 127)

Anna Pavlovna m. William II of the Netherlands *d. 1849* (❧ page 139)

Frederick William III (1770–1840)

KING OF PRUSSIA (1797–1840)

House of Hohenzollern

Knowing he lacked the strength of character to push through the reforms Prussia needed, Frederick William passed the responsibility to a series of well-chosen ministers. The big issue of his reign was the threat posed by revolutionary France. Frederick William at first avoided involvement in the wars but by 1804 Napoleon's forces were at his door and he had no choice but to defend Prussia against invasion.

He was famously defeated in the Battle of Jena in 1806, and the subsequent peace brought Prussia to its knees before France. Napoleon forced Frederick's abandonment of his old alliance with Russia and insisted that a Prussian force be sent to support his campaign in the east. The leaders of this force thought better and negotiated terms with Tsar Alexander I. Prussia once again turned its back on the French and assisted Russia in its victory over Napoleon. To cement the alliance Frederick William agreed to the marriage of his daughter Charlotte to the tsar's brother Nicholas (later Nicholas I).

Royal Connections

Grandsons: Alexander II of Russia *d. 1881* (⚜ page 147),
Frederick III of Germany *d. 1888* (⚜ page 152)

Married

Louise of Mecklenburg-Strelitz *d. 1810*

Children

Frederick William IV of Prussia *d. 1861* (⚜ page 140)
William I of Germany *d. 1888* (⚜ page 152)
Charlotte m. Nicholas I of Russia *d. 1855* (⚜ page 127)

Frederick William III of Prussia.

1800-1899
The House of Hanover

George IV to Victoria

Alexander I (1777–1825)

TSAR OF RUSSIA (1801–21)

House of Romanov

Catherine the Great's preferred successor was her grandson Alexander, and she brought him up at her court where he could be educated accordingly. Despite these plans, Alexander had to wait for his father's reign to run its course before he could take the crown. Understanding the resentment that had led to Paul's murder (it is believed that he knew of the planned assassination although he played no part in it), Alexander began to rectify some of the unpopular policies introduced in his predecessor's reign. Although he failed to make much impact, he at least attempted to improve the situation for the serfs, as well as modernising the education system.

His foreign policy vacillated between periods of support for and opposition to Napoleon, but though defeated at Austerlitz in 1805 he successfully resisted the great invasion of 1812 and was a leader of the coalition that eventually brought down Napoleon. In post-Napoleonic Europe he was the protagonist of the Holy Alliance, an organisation created ostensibly to protect Christian principles in Europe and which eventually found the support of most European monarchs. His religious fervour characterised the rest of his reign – so much so that on his death rumours abounded that he had simply gone to live as a hermit in Siberia.

Royal Connections

Nephew: Alexander II of Russia *d. 1881* (✤ page 147)

Married

Louise of Baden *d. 1826*

Children

None surviving

Alexander I grew increasingly despotic as his reign progressed.

Napoleon Bonaparte, Emperor of the French.

Napoleon I (1769–1821)

EMPEROR OF THE FRENCH (1804–15)

House of Bonaparte

Napoleon was born in Corsica the year after France acquired the island, and received the military education of a French nobleman. Initially he saw the French Revolution as a chance to return to Corsica, but his artillery skills led to a meteoric rise in the French army, and he made his name as a republican general, defeating the Austrians in Italy in 1796–97. Seizing control of the republic in 1799, he resolved

the problems bequeathed by the Revolution and in 1804 was proclaimed hereditary emperor on the results of a referendum.

Between 1805 and 1807 he fought the Austrians, Russians and Prussians and defeated them all. Only the British, secure beyond the seas, stood out against him. But his wife Josephine was too old to have children, and he wanted to found a dynasty. He therefore used his victory in a further war against the Austrians as an opportunity to divorce her and marry the Austrian emperor's daughter, by whom he had a son. Within two years, however, his decline and fall had begun, with the disastrous invasion of Russia. In the aftermath of his retreat from Moscow, the German powers (including his father-in-law) combined against him and he was driven back into France, where he abdicated. He was given the island of Elba as a kingdom, while Louis XVIII brought Bourbon rule back to France. Napoleon's escape from Elba, and his final 'hundred days' of rule in France, were brought to an end by defeat at Waterloo at the hands of the British Duke of Wellington. The Napoleonic Wars were over. The 'little general' himself was exiled to the island of St Helena for the rest of his life. The house of Bonaparte did not die with him, however, and it was some years before France was finally rid of Napoleon's heirs.

Royal Connections

Father-in-law: Holy Roman Emperor Francis II *d. 1835* (⚜ page 104)

Married

1. Josephine de Beauharnais *d. 1814*
2. Marie Louise of Parma *d. 1847*

Children

Napoleon II of France *d. 1832* (⚜ page 121)

Louis Bonaparte (1778–1846)

KING OF HOLLAND (1806–10)

As Napoleon I seized territories all across Europe, he distributed their government among his family members. His younger brother Louis was proclaimed King of Holland in 1806. Sympathetically defending the country's interests rather than those of his brother, he was eventually deposed by Napoleon. Louis' son later ruled France as Napoleon III.

a revolution in 1820, but the reactionary king turned ironically to France for military support, and used it to pursue a campaign of ruthless repression.

Despite four marriages, two of them with his own nieces, Ferdinand had only two surviving children – both girls. His death in 1833 left the country in the same turmoil as his reign had witnessed, with his three-year-old daughter set to succeed him.

Royal Connections

Cousin: Holy Roman Emperor Francis II *d. 1835* (❧ page 104)

Nephews: Peter IV of Portugal *d. 1834* (❧ page 122),

Michael I of Portugal *d. 1866* (❧ page 128)

Married

1. Maria Antoinetta of the Two Sicilies *d. 1806*

2. Maria Isabel of Braganza *d. 1818*

3. Maria Josepha of Saxony *d. 1829*

4. Maria Christina of Bourbon-Two Sicilies *d. 1878*

Children

Isabella II of Spain *d. 1904* (❧ page 134)

Ferdinand VII (1784–1833)

KING OF SPAIN (1808–33)

House of Bourbon

Ferdinand had always disliked his father's chief minister Godoy, and before Charles's abdication he began plotting to gain favour with the French emperor Napoleon. His plans were uncovered and he was arrested on the orders of his father. Although he was quickly released and restored to favour, the incident destabilised the already weak Spanish monarchy. It was not a difficult task for the wily Napoleon to manipulate them. Shortly after Charles's abdication, Napoleon lured Ferdinand across the border into French territory and forced him to relinquish his crown. Napoleon's brother Joseph was proclaimed king, and for the next five years Ferdinand was held captive in France.

He retained strong support in Spain and the liberal factions insisted on a reformed constitution, which was proclaimed in 1812. When Ferdinand was finally restored to his throne he turned his back on his supporters and rejected the constitution. It was brought back after

Joseph I Napoleon (1768–1844)

KING OF SPAIN (1808–13)

After Napoleon I had masterminded the abdication of both Charles IV and his son Ferdinand VII, he placed his own elder brother on the Spanish throne. Despite such efforts to achieve popularity as abandoning the Spanish Inquisition, Joseph was a foreigner dependent on his brother's army and was never taken to the hearts of the Spanish people. He abdicated after the French defeat at the Battle of Vitoria, and Ferdinand was reinstated.

Frederick VI was first cousins with George IV and William IV of Great Britain.

Royal Connections

Cousins: George IV of Great Britain and Ireland *d. 1830* (♣ page 124),

William IV of Great Britain and Ireland *d. 1837* (♣ page 128)

Married

Marie Sophie of Hesse-Kassel *d. 1852*

Children

Wilhelmine m. Frederick VII of Denmark *d. 1863* (♣ page 142)

Frederick VI (1768–1839)

KING OF DENMARK (1808–39),

KING OF NORWAY (1808–14)

House of Oldenburg

As Christian VII descended into insanity, the government of Denmark and Norway fell increasingly to his son Frederick and in 1784 he was formally acknowledged regent. After the disasters associated with his father's reliance on his physician and councillor Struensee, Frederick chose his confidants more carefully. He relied greatly on Andreas Peter Bernstorff, the nephew of Christian's earlier chief minister, and together they planned a series of liberal reforms.

As the rest of Europe erupted into the French revolutionary wars Frederick hoped to maintain Denmark's neutrality. The one thorn in his side was Britain, to whose ruling family he was closely related. But although his exiled mother was sister to King George III, the familial connection did not protect neutral Danish shipping from attack by the Royal Navy, and later the Danish fleet was destroyed in Copenhagen itself to ensure continued British access to the Baltic. Denmark had little alternative but to turn to Napoleon. Frederick thus shared in France's downfall and was punished in 1813 by the loss of Norway to Sweden in the Congress of Vienna. Disillusioned, he never returned to the liberal ideologies of his regency and became increasingly autocratic. With no sons to succeed him, the throne passed to his nephew Christian VIII on his death.

Charles XIII (1748–1818)

KING OF SWEDEN (1809–18),

KING OF NORWAY (AS CHARLES II, 1814–18)

House of Holstein-Gottorp

C harles had acted as regent during the minority of his nephew Gustav IV Adolf, and was elected king by the Riksdag on Gustav's abdication in 1809. He had been married in 1774, and his queen, Hedvig of Holstein-Gottorp, was also his cousin. She was vivacious and clever and, like her husband, conducted several affairs. Hedvig's greatest secret desire was to wield more power, but this was not an idea that the nobles would even entertain. By the time Charles came to the throne he was showing signs of early senility and, to the disappointment of the queen, the reins of government were handed to Jean-Baptiste Bernadotte, a French marshall.

Royal Connections

Brother: Gustav III of Sweden *d. 1792* (⚜ page 97)

Uncle: Frederick II of Prussia *d. 1786* (⚜ page 81)

Married

Hedvig Elizabeth Charlotte of Holstein-Gottorp *d. 1818*

Children

None surviving

Charles XIII presided over Sweden's acquisition of Norway from Denmark.

William I (1772–1843)

KING OF THE NETHERLANDS (1815–1840)

House of Orange-Nassau

William's father was the stadtholder William V, Prince of Orange, and he grew up well-educated in administrative affairs. He married his cousin the Prussian princess Wilhelmine in 1791, and took his family to England when the French invaded the Dutch Republic four years later. He returned in 1813, and by the Congress of Vienna was granted the title King of the Netherlands, which at that time included Belgium and Luxembourg. By the end of his reign, however, Belgium at least had won its independence. William's unwillingness to conform to a liberal constitution eventually forced his abdication in favour of his eldest son.

Royal Connections

Father-in-law: Frederick William II of Prussia

d. 1797 (✤ page 101)

Married

Wilhelmine of Prussia *d. 1837*

Children

William II of the Netherlands *d. 1849* (✤ page 139)

William I was the first ruler of the new kingdom of the Netherlands, created in 1815.

Louis XVIII (1755–1824)

KING OF FRANCE (1814–24)

House of Bourbon

The younger brother of Louis XVI had fled France in 1791, at the same moment the ill-fated king himself attempted to escape. He spent some time at the courts of several royalist supporting monarchs in Europe before settling in England in 1807. When the allies emerged victorious from the Napoleonic wars, Louis returned in triumph to France and was hastily proclaimed king (although Louis himself always dated his reign from 1795, the death of his nephew Louis XVII).

In trying to please everyone, Louis ended up pleasing no one, and was forced into exile once more by the return of Napoleon in 1815. After Waterloo Louis returned 'in the allies' baggage train' to an occupied kingdom that had lost all the territorial gains of a generation. By patience and caution he gradually restored France's position as a great power, but was unable to dampen the bitter internal political antagonisms resulting from years of revolution. Childless, he was succeeded by his much less diplomatic younger brother, who squandered the dynasty's remaining political capital.

The reign of Louis XVIII was briefly interrupted by the return of Napoleon to the French throne.

Royal Connections

Grandfathers: Louis XV of France *d. 1774* (🪷 page 70),
Augustus III of Poland *d. 1763* (🪷 page 78)

Married

Marie Josephine Louise of Savoy *d. 1810*

Children

None

Napoleon II (1811–32)

EMPEROR OF THE FRENCH (1815)

During the reign of Louis XVIII, Napoleon returned to rule France for a period known as the 'hundred days'. He finally abdicated in favour of his infant son Napoleon II in 1815, but the reign was short-lived. The allies banished Napoleon I and his son was taken to Austria.

John VI was forced to take up arms against his sons after they conspired to overthrow his rule in Brazil.

John VI (1767–1826)
KING OF PORTUGAL (1816–26)
House of Braganza

John became heir to the Portuguese throne on the death of his elder brother José from smallpox in 1788. His mother Maria I was already displaying signs of mental instability and four years later John was declared regent. When the French invaded Portugal in 1807 John and his family fled to Brazil. His sons Michael and Peter conspired to free Brazil from their father's rule and it was declared independent in 1825, the year before John's death.

Royal Connections

Father-in-law: Charles IV of Spain *d. 1819* (❧ page 102)

Granddaughter: Maria II of Portugal *d. 1853* (❧ page 127)

Married

Charlotte of Spain *d. 1830*

Children

Maria Isabel m. Ferdinand VII of Spain *d. 1833* (❧ page 116)

Peter IV of Portugal *d. 1834* (❧ page 122)

Michael I of Portugal *d. 1866* (❧ page 128)

Peter IV (1798–1834)
KING OF PORTUGAL (1826)

Peter IV – better known as Peter I of Brazil – was briefly acknowledged king of Portugal on the death of John VI, but he chose to pass the crown to his young daughter Maria II on condition that she marry her uncle, Peter's brother Michael, and rule with him. Michael reneged on his agreement, sparking the War of the Two Brothers.

Charles XIV John (1763–1844)

KING OF SWEDEN AND NORWAY (1818–44)

House of Bernadotte

Jean-Baptiste Bernadotte was born and grew up in France. He sided with the revolutionaries in 1789 and became a high-ranking officer in the revolutionary army. In 1798 he married Désirée Clary, the first love of Napoleon Bonaparte, and whose sister had married Napoleon's brother Joseph. This familial connection proved advantageous for Bernadotte, who flourished during the era of the French empire despite Napoleon's mistrust. However, his failures at the Battle of Wagram in 1809 marked the end of his military career.

The following year he was invited by the Swedish Riksdag to become its crown prince, as the ageing Charles XIII had no heir. His acceptance of this role and his associated desire to annexe Norway from Denmark necessitated a political about-face, and he gathered an army to fight Napoleon. He took part in the victory at Leipzig in 1813, and the following year succeeded in claiming Norway. Four years later he acceded the throne and took the name Charles XIV John. His reign passed peacefully and he was popular with the people of his adopted country.

Royal Connections

Grandsons: Charles XV of Sweden and Norway *d. 1872* (♣ page 148),
Oscar II of Sweden and Norway *d. 1907* (⚜ page 157)

Married

Désirée Clary *d. 1860*

Children

Oscar I of Sweden and Norway *d. 1859* (♣ page 141)

Jean-Baptiste Bernadotte, who became king of Sweden and Norway.

George IV (1762–1830)

KING OF GREAT BRITAIN AND IRELAND (1820–30)

House of Hanover

George endured a poor relationship with his father, George III, and it was with ill-disguised glee that he assumed the mantle of regent on the old king's final descent into insanity. His marriage to his first cousin Caroline of Brunswick was not a happy union, and technically bigamous, since he had secretly married Maria Fitzherbert 10 years previously. The queen's only child Charlotte died in 1817. His attempt to divorce Queen Caroline in 1820 brought him widespread ridicule and unpopularity, and his political vacillations over matters such as Catholic Emancipation did little to restore his prestige.

His tastes were extravagant, and his main monuments were his additions to the royal art collections and lavish buildings at Brighton, Windsor and Buckingham Palace, identified as setting the 'Regency' style.

Royal Connections

Cousin: Frederick VI of Denmark and Norway *d. 1839* (♣ page 118)

Niece: Victoria of Great Britain and Ireland *d. 1901* (♣ page 137)

Married

Caroline of Brunswick *d. 1821*

Children

Charlotte Augusta of Wales *d. 1817*

George IV in his decadent youth; in his old age he became corpulent and delusional.

Charles X (1757–1836)

KING OF FRANCE (1824–30)
House of Bourbon

Charles was the third of Louis XV's grandsons to sit on the French throne, and the last of the direct Bourbon line. Before the Revolution the spendthrift and dissolute lifestyle of the then Count d'Anjou represented everything the revolutionaries would come to detest about the court of Versailles. With his brother, who later became Louis XVIII, Charles spent many years in exile during the revolutionary and Napoleonic wars, but returned to France at their conclusion as heir-presumptive to the childless king. He always opposed the moderation of Louis XVIII, and when he succeeded to the throne, he worked to overturn the achievements of the Revolution and Napoleonic Empire. Now pious and devout, he sought to promote the authority of the church, restore the pre-eminence of the old nobility, and restrict civil and political liberties, Attempts to curb parliament and the press caused a public outcry and he was forced to abdicate on behalf of himself and his heirs in the Revolution of July 1830.

Royal Connections
Grandfathers: Louis XV of France *d. 1774* (♣ page 70),
Augustus III of Poland *d. 1763* (♣ page 78)
Brothers: Louis XVI of France *d. 1793* (♣ page 99),
Louis XVIII *d. 1824* (♣ page 121)

Married
Maria Theresa of Savoy *d. 1805*

Children
Louis-Antoine of France *d. 1844* (♣ page 125)

Charles X followed his two brothers, Louis XVI and Louis XVIII, to the throne of France.

Louis-Antoine (1775–1844)

KING OF FRANCE (1830)

The shortest-reigning king in the history of France, Louis-Antoine held the title for 20 minutes after his father's abdication in 1830. His wife (his first cousin Maria Theresa Charlotte, Duchess of Angoulême, daughter of Louis XVI and Marie Antoinette) begged him not to sign his own abdication papers, but he had little choice and the legitimist claim to the throne passed to his nephew Henry Count of Chambord (♣ page 131).

Nicholas I (1796–1855)

TSAR OF RUSSIA (1825–55)

House of Romanov

Nicholas I succeeded his childless brother, Alexander I, in 1825. His reign began with the abortive Decembrist uprising of army officers fearful of his reactionary reputation. Its failure only increased these inclinations. The reign saw the suppression of several uprisings in neighbouring countries, including Poland and Hungary, and it ended drifting into the Crimean War. He made some attempts to limit the power of landowners over their serfs, but the tsar's methods were dictatorial and he feared any kind of liberal expression. His strict censorship laws and the religious persecution he permitted ensured his unpopularity. He left his son and successor a legacy of autocracy and international war.

Royal Connections

Father-in-law: Frederick William III of Prussia

d. 1840 (❧ page 108)

Grandmother: Catherine II of Russia

d. 1796 (❧ page 92)

Married

Charlotte of Prussia *d. 1860*

Children

Alexander II of Russia *d. 1881* (❧ page 147)

When she finally claimed her throne, Maria gained a reputation for kindness and tolerance.

Maria II (1819–53)

QUEEN OF PORTUGAL (1834–53)

House of Braganza

Maria was only seven years old when her father granted a constitutional charter and abdicated in her favour. She was betrothed to her uncle, Michael, who was appointed regent of Portugal. By the time Maria arrived in Portugal from Brazil, however, Michael had usurped the throne.

It was several years before Maria's father managed to restore her rights. A kindly woman with a reputation as a good wife and mother, Maria had 11 children by her second husband. She died giving birth to the last of these, and was succeeded by the first – Peter V.

Royal Connections

Grandfather: Holy Roman Emperor Francis II

d. 1835 (❧ page 104)

Uncle: Michael I of Portugal *d. 1866*

(❧ page 128)

Married

1. Auguste Charles of Leuchtenberg *d. 1835*

2. Ferdinand of Saxe-Coburg-Gotha *d. 1836*

Children

Peter V of Portugal *d. 1861* (❧ page 146)

Louis I of Portugal *d. 1889* (❧ page 151)

Michael I
(1802–66)

KING OF PORTUGAL
(1828–34)

House of Braganza

Michael broke the agreement he had made with his brother Peter IV on the latter's abdication in 1826. He abandoned the charter that had been drawn up between them, which allowed him the regency of his niece (and intended wife) Maria, and began to rule Portugal with absolute power. Peter gathered his forces and in the campaign that became known as the War of the Two Brothers, defeated Michael and forced his exile from Portugal. Michael continued to rally support throughout and beyond Maria's reign.

Royal Connections

Niece: Maria II of Portugal *d. 1853* (⚜ page 127)

Married

Adelaide of Löwenstein-Wertheim-Rosenberg *d. 1909*

Children

Michael II, Duke of Braganza *d. 1927*

William IV
(1765–1837)

KING OF GREAT BRITAIN
AND IRELAND (1830–37)

House of Hanover

As the third son of George II, the 'Sailor King' William had never entertained the idea of succeeding to the throne, and spent his youth in the navy. But the death of his eldest brother Frederick and that of his niece Charlotte, daughter of George IV, forced him into the limelight. Despite having a large family by his mistress, he recognised the need to produce legitimate heirs and to that end married Adelaide of Saxe-Meinigen in 1818. None of their children survived infancy, but the British people took the queen to their hearts anyway. William was not a natural ruler, but he successfully rode the crisis of the parliamentary Reform Bill in 1831–32 and was succeeded by his niece Victoria, the last of the Hanoverians.

Royal Connections

Cousin: Frederick VI of Denmark and Norway *d. 1839* (⚜ page 118)

Niece: Victoria of Great Britain and Ireland *d. 1901* (⚜ page 137)

Married

Adelaide of Saxe-Meinigen *d. 1849*

Children

None legitimate

Louis-Philippe (1773–1850)

KING OF THE FRENCH (1830–48)

House of Bourbon-Orléans

Louis-Philippe was the eldest son of Philip, Duke of Orléans. He had revolutionary sympathies, and fought in the revolutionary armies in 1792. A year later he deserted and went into hiding while the revolutionary and Napoleonic Wars played out.

He returned to France when the monarchy was restored in 1814. After the July Revolution in 1830, when Charles and his heirs were disinherited, Louis-Philippe was chosen to be King of the French. Painfully aware of the fragile political peace in his country, the new Citizen King walked a careful line, trying to reconcile the extremes of French politics. Unable to maintain the middle ground to which he always aspired, Louis-Philippe abdicated in 1848.

Married

Maria Amalia of the Two Sicilies *d. 1866*

Children

Crown Prince Ferdinand Philippe *d. 1842*

Henry, Count of Chambord (1820–83)

KING OF FRANCE (1830)

Before Louis-Philippe was officially declared king, Chambord spent a week as Henry V, after his grandfather Charles X and the 20-minute king, his uncle Louis-Antoine, abdicated. After seven days, the National Assembly declared that the direct line of Charles X had forfeited its rights, and proclaimed his distant cousin the rightful heir.

Otto I (1815–67)

KING OF GREECE (1838–62)
House of Wittelsbach

On 1832 the great powers of Britain and France agreed that Otto, the second son of Ludwig I of Bavaria, descended from Greek royal bloodlines, should become king of the newly independent Greece.

Otto was 18 when he landed in Greece ready to assume his responsibilities, and he soon discovered that the Greeks were displeased with the Great Powers' selection. His Bavarian birth and his staunch Catholicism alienated his new subjects. Although he made great efforts to rule as an absolute king, the young monarchy fell foul of more than one military coup, forcing upon the king a revised constitution that gave his subjects more power in government. Otto also managed to alienate the very powers that had granted his position by breaking a rule of his appointment and attacking the Ottoman Turks. The swift intervention of France and Britain reminded the king not to bite the hand that feeds.

His downfall came with a final attempt to abandon the constitution in 1863, during which the military forced his deposition. Otto returned to Bavaria with his wife, and died there four years later.

Married
Amalia of Oldenburg *d. 1875*

Children
None

Otto I – the first king of Greece.

Isabella's religious fervour and her authoritarian outlook alienated her people and her government and forced her into exile.

Isabella II (1830–1904)

QUEEN OF SPAIN (1838–68)

House of Bourbon

Isabella was the daughter of Ferdinand VII and his wife Maria Christina (her uncle both by birth and marriage). Despite four marriages Ferdinand had been unable to produce a male heir and he thus persuaded the Cortes to allow him to set aside Salic Law, which prohibited inheritance through the female line, and named Isabella his heir. This provoked the Carlist wars, through which Isabella's uncle Charles, son of Charles IV, disputed her claim.

She was only three when her father died and her mother – and briefly the army general Espartes – acted as regents until 1843, at which time Isabella was deemed to be of age. Three years later she was forced to marry her cousin, Francis. She had 12 children by him but only four survived, including the future Alfonso XII. Isabella's sister Louisa married a son of Louis-Philippe of France. These two unions were in contravention of an existing agreement between France and England, reaffirming as they did ties between France and Spain, and for a time the entente between the two nations hung in the balance.

Isabella was deposed in 1868 after years of political factionalism and insurrections. She fled to France and two years later she officially renounced her position and passed the crown to her son.

Royal Connections

Grandson: Alfonso XIII *d. 1941* (⚜ page 161)

Married

Francis of Spain *d. 1902*

Children

Alfonso XII of Spain *d. 1885* (⚜ page 158)

Ferdinand I (1793–1875)

EMPEROR OF AUSTRIA, KING OF HUNGARY (1830–48)
House of Habsburg-Lorraine

Despite Ferdinand's mental instability and physical problems (he suffered from epilepsy) his father, Emperor Francis II, insisted that he remain heir to the thrones of Austria, Hungary and Bohemia. His disabilities meant that for the duration of his reign his territories were governed by the council, led by Klemens von Metternich. When revolution was staged in Vienna in 1848, Ferdinand felt it wise to abdicate and allow his nephew Francis Joseph to take over.

Royal Connections

Father: Holy Roman Emperor Francis II *d. 1835* (❧ page 104)

Married

Maria Anna of Sardinia *d. 1884*

Children

None

Ferdinand I was not considered fit to rule and government lay in the hands of his ministers.

Victoria (1819–1901)

QUEEN OF GREAT BRITAIN AND
IRELAND (1837–1901)
House of Hanover

Victoria's reign was the longest of any British monarch, and she presided over the peak of British power and prestige. Domestically there were reforms that steadily widened political participation, while economically the kingdom gloried in being the 'workshop of the world'. Internationally Victoria stood as a symbolic figurehead for the British Empire, which controlled and influenced one-fifth of the globe.

In fact, the power of the monarchy declined substantially during the 63 years of Victoria's reign. True government lay in the hands of ministers, the most notable of whom were Benjamin Disraeli (whom the queen much admired) and William Gladstone (whom she disliked). But a decline in power did not mean a decline in grandeur, and the reign was characterised by imperial pageantry on a large scale. Despite this, the queen was perceived to be very human – a devoted wife and loving mother. Her protracted period of withdrawal after the death of her beloved husband Prince Albert incited praise and sympathy to begin with, although later rumblings about her neglect of duties forced a return to public life much against her will.

By the end of her reign Victoria was known as the Grandmother of Europe. The dynastic intermarriages of her children had touched many royal families on the continent, including the German Empire, Denmark, Prussia and Russia. As the twentieth century began, events that would pit her descendants one against the other with tragic consequences began to take shape on the world stage.

Royal Connections

Uncles: George IV of Great Britain and Ireland *d. 1830* (❧ page 124),
William IV of Great Britain and Ireland *d. 1837* (❧ page 128)
Grandsons: William II of Germany *d. 1941* (❧ page 162),
George V of Great Britain and Ireland *d. 1936* (❧ page 174)

Married

Albert of Saxe-Coburg-Gotha *d. 1861*

Children

Victoria m. Frederick III of Germany *d. 1888* (❧ page 152)
Edward VII of Great Britain and Ireland *d. 1910* (❧ page 169)

Victoria had 11 children, whose marriages with other European royalty expanded and strengthened Britain's international ties.

Christian VIII (1786–1848)

KING OF DENMARK (1839–48), KING OF NORWAY (1814)

House of Oldenburg

Christian had been earmarked as successor to Frederick VI for many years before he finally began to play a part in state affairs, and when he did it was on a tide of bad fortune. When Norway was ceded to Sweden at the conclusion of the Napoleonic Wars, Christian was sent to Norway to stir up popularity for the Danish king. He took over leadership of the Norwegian Independence Party and in 1814 was elected king, but was ousted after just a few months in favour of Charles XIII.

Returning to Denmark he was forced to simply bide his time waiting for the old king to die. His democratic principles were not popular, so shunned from court, he and his second wife Caroline Amalia contented themselves with artistic and scientific pursuits in a social circle of their own making. Christian's democratic leanings did not survive his eventual assumption of power in 1839 and he systematically blocked any liberal reforms put forward. Frederick's long life denied his successor the opportunity to make any kind of long-lasting impact. He died after less than 10 years and was succeeded by his son Frederick VII.

Christian VIII's first marriage, to his cousin Charlotte of Mecklenburg-Schwerin, was annulled in 1810 and he married Caroline Amlia five years later.

Royal Connections

Uncle: Christian VII of Denmark *d. 1808* (✤ page 96)

Married

1. Charlotte Frederika of Mecklenburg-Schwerin *d. 1840*
2. Caroline Amalia of Augstenburg *d. 1881*

Children

Frederick VII of Denmark *d. 1863* (✤ page 142)

William II (1792–1849)

KING OF THE NETHERLANDS (1840–49)

House of Orange-Nassau

Willliam II was the son of William I of the Netherlands and his wife, the princess of Prussia Wilhelmina. Trained in the military, he participated in the Napoleonic Wars and was wounded at the Battle of Waterloo. He had spent time in exile in England and was briefly considered as a husband for Charlotte, the only child of George IV, but the princess expressed a distaste for William and instead he married Anna Pavlovna, daughter of Paul I of Russia, thus cementing the alliance between the countries. As king he continued his father's conservative policies, but witnessing the overthrow of the French monarchy after widespread insurrections in 1848, he began to employ a more liberal approach. He died unexpectedly the following year.

Royal Connections

Uncle: Frederick William III of Prussia *d. 1840* (♣ page 108)

Brothers-in-law: Alexander I of Russia *d. 1825* (♣ page 112),

Nicholas I of Russia *d. 1855* (♣ page 127)

Married

Anna Pavlovna of Russia *d. 1965*

Children

William III of the Netherlands *d. 1890* (♣ page 144)

William II and his Russian wife had five children, including the future William III.

Frederick William IV (1795–1861)

KING OF PRUSSIA (1840–61)

House of Hohenzollern

Frederick William conceived romantic plans for a return to the patriarchal monarchy and social systems of the medieval period in Prussia. However, the 1848 revolutions across the continent encapsulated a desire for modernisation and limits to monarchical power. Frederick William at first acquiesced, but later stood firm against revolutionary thinking and imposed a conservative constitution in his country.

Although he was keen to see the German states united under Prussian leadership, Frederick William refused the offer to make him king of Germany, believing that an elected group had no authority to bargain with a divinely appointed monarch. Mental illness caused his withdrawal from public life in 1857, and Prussia came under the regency of his brother William. It was he who became the first German Emperor.

Royal Connections

Nephew: Frederick III of Germany *d. 1888* ( page 152)

Married

Elisabeth Ludovika of Bavaria *d. 1873*

Children

None

Oscar I (1799–1859)

KING OF SWEDEN AND NORWAY (1844–59)

House of Bernadotte

T he son of Charles XIV, the first Bernadotte king of Sweden, Oscar had been brought up understanding the intricacies of social policy; he grasped this so well that his father began to view him as a threat when he started colluding with the liberals in Norway. His experience stood him in good stead when he inherited the throne in 1844. Oscar had objected to his father's despotic tendencies and the liberals had high hopes of reform when he took over. However, Oscar preferred to tread the middle ground and pursued moderate policies that upset the more radical of his former supporters.

He had long hoped for a union between Sweden, Norway and Denmark – and established an equality between his two realms – but the enmity that had existed for centuries between the Swedish and the Danes was not easily forgotten and he was forced to abandon these plans. The birth of four strong sons, however, secured the future of the House of Bernadotte.

Royal Connections

Grandson: Gustav V of Sweden *d. 1950* (⚜ page 173)

Married

Josephine of Leuchtenberg *d. 1876*

Children

Charles XV of Sweden and Norway *d. 1872* (⚜ page 148)

Oscar II of Sweden and Norway *d. 1907* (⚜ page 157)

Oscar was famous for the book he wrote on reforms in criminal law and the prison system.

The Oldenburg line was finally extinguished with the death of Frederick VII of Denmark.

Frederick VII (1808–63)

KING OF DENMARK (1848–63)
House of Oldenburg

Frederick, the last of the Oldenburg kings of Denmark, was a popular monarch. He gained a reputation for justice and sympathy with his subjects and, renouncing absolutism in favour of constitutional monarchy, established a parliament in Denmark for the first time.

Frederick was married three times, but even before he succeeded the throne there were suspicions that he was sterile and he never produced a child. War broke out after his death over the rights to the crown.

Royal Connections
Father: Christian VIII of Denmark *d. 1848* (✤ page 138)

Married
1. Wilhelmine Marie of Denmark *d. 1891*

2. Caroline Charlotte of Mecklenburg-Strelitz *d. 1876*

3. Louise Rasmussen *d. 1874*

Children
None

Francis Joseph I (1830–1916)

EMPEROR OF AUSTRIA (1848–1916),

KING OF HUNGARY (1867–1916)

House of Habsburg

Francis Joseph I enjoyed a long but tragic reign.

The 68-year reign of Francis Joseph was one of the longest in European history. It was framed by two events of continent-wide significance – he became emperor during the 1848 revolutions, which had resulted in his uncle's abdication, and he died at the height of the First World War, a conflict triggered by his own ministers.

From the start he attempted to stabilise his dominions after the revolutions by ruling with a firm absolutist hand, but his methods alienated many of his subjects and he faced rebellions across the empire. The most significant of these was focused in Hungary, and Francis Joseph eventually responded by creating the dual monarchy of Austria-Hungary in 1867. After defeat by Prussia in the Seven Weeks' War (1866) he signed an agreement with the victor (and by association most of the German states), that later developed into the Triple Alliance with the addition of Italy. When Francis Joseph's nephew and heir presumptive Francis Ferdinand was murdered in Serbia in 1914, the Austrian emperor delivered an ultimatum that set the wheels in motion for global war.

Francis Joseph's personal life was beset with tragedy. In 1867 his brother Maximilian was executed in Mexico after an abortive attempt to install him as emperor. In 1889 his son and heir, Crown Prince Rudolf, died in suspicious circumstances that may have been murder or more probably a suicide pact with his lover Mary Vetsera. In 1898, his wife Elisabeth was assassinated. With no sons to succeed him and his nephew killed, the throne passed to his great-nephew Charles.

Royal Connections

Grandfather: Holy Roman Emperor Leopold II *d. 1792* (♣ page 103)

Married

Elisabeth of Bavaria *d. 1898*

Children

Crown Prince Rudolf *d. 1889*

William III (1817–90)

KING OF THE NETHERLANDS (1849–90)

House of Orange-Nassau

William's father, William II, had agreed to a liberal constitution in the Netherlands shortly before his death – a decision that his son tried to overturn almost immediately on his accession. Despite the unrest of his predecessor's reign, William's constitutional rule seems to have earned the trust and respect of his parliament and his people.

His attempts to exert control over Luxembourg briefly threatened stability abroad, but he ultimately acquiesced to the demands of his Prussian relatives that the area should be independent. His three sons – William, Maurice and Alexander – predeceased him, and on his death the throne passed to his daughter Wilhelmina.

Royal Connections

Uncles: Alexander I of Russia *d. 1825* (page 112),
Nicholas I of Russia *d. 1855* (page 127)
Granddaughter: Juliana of the Netherlands *d. 1980* (page 184)

Married

1. Sophie of Württemburg *d. 1877*
2. Emma of Waldeck and Pyrmont *d. 1934*

Children

Wilhelmina of the Netherlands *d. 1962* (page 164)

Napoleon III (1808–73)

EMPEROR OF THE FRENCH (1852–70)

House of Bonaparte

Louis-Napoleon Bonaparte was the third son of Napoleon's brother Louis. After his uncle's exile, Louis Napoleon spent most of his life abroad until the revolution of 1848 brought him hastening back to France to secure election to the National Assembly. Disillusioned by the ineffectiveness of the Second Republic that followed the abdication of Louis-Philippe, the French elected Louis-Napoleon as president. Limited to one term in this role by the constitution, he began at once to consolidate his position. It was not difficult to stage a coup that ensured his future as ruler – the very name Bonaparte reminded the people of the glory days of the Empire – and in 1852 he seized hereditary power as Emperor of the French under the name Napoleon III. His rule was dictatorial at first, but growing unrest later forced him to employ more liberal policies. Internationally Napoleon III brought France into the Crimean War and promoted the unification of Italy, but in 1870 he allowed his country to be dragged into war against Prussia. The Franco-Prussian War ended in disaster. Napoleon's defeat at the Battle of Sedan resulted in demands for his removal and his abdication that same year marked the end of the last monarchy in France.

Royal Connections

Uncle: Napoleon I *d. 1821* (❧ page 115)

Married

Eugenie of Montijo *d. 1920*

Children

Prince Imperial Napoleon Eugene *d. 1879*

France's last monarch, Napoleon III.

Peter V of Portugal.

Peter V (1837–1861)

KING OF PORTUGAL (1853–61)

House of Braganza-Saxe-Coburg-Gotha

After the turmoil that had characterised the reigns of his predecessors, most notably the succession wars fought between his grandfather Peter IV and his great-uncle Michael I, Peter brought renewed calm to Portugal. Intelligent and with a great love of culture, he worked hard to improve the country's infrastructure – including the establishment of railways and health facilities – as well as abolishing slavery in his realm.

Royal Connections

Brother: Louis I of Portugal *d. 1889* (⚜ page 151)

Married

Stephanie of Hohenzollern-Sigmaringen *d. 1859*

Children

None

Alexander II (1818–81)

TSAR OF RUSSIA (1855–81)

House of Romanov

Alexander inherited his autocratic principles from his father Nicholas I, and although he initially showed signs of having learned the lessons of his predecessors, he never quite broke free of the belief that the upper echelons of the Russian class structure were a threat to the stability of the kingdom.

Alexander came to the throne during the Crimean War, instigated by Nicholas and his plans for expansion at the expense of the Turkish Empire. By this time it had drawn in several other European powers and Alexander was forced to negotiate what amounted to defeat for Russia. It opened his eyes to how far his country was lacking in modern infrastructure compared with neighbouring powers. His solution was swift and decisive – an extensive overhaul of all political, administrative and domestic systems, from education to government. He finally fulfilled the empty promises of his forebears and granted the serfs their freedom, for which he earned himself the nickname 'The Liberator'. While his reforms appeared to be sweeping, radicals still felt his policy too moderate and civil unrest finally made Alexander resort to force, which cost him his life. Alexander was assassinated by a member of the terrorist People's Will movement in 1881.

Alexander II of Russia earned the name 'The Liberator'.

Royal Connections

Grandson: Nicholas II of Russia *d. 1918* (✣ page 165)

Married

Maria Alexandrovna *d. 1880*

Children

Alexander III of Russia *d. 1894* (✣ page 160)

Charles XV (1826–72)

KING OF SWEDEN AND NORWAY (1859–72)

House of Bernadotte

A popular king, Charles XV's reign was notable for his strict adherence to the laws of constitutional monarchy and his widespread reforms, including revisions to religious and criminal law and the restructuring of the Riksdag. He showed both tolerance and friendship towards Sweden's old enemy Denmark and enjoyed a warm relationship with that country's king, Frederick VII. He believed that the three Scandinavian kingdoms should be united if not politically, at least in the face they presented to the rest of the world. Intelligent, cultured and with a strong sense of his responsibilities, Charles was greatly mourned on his death.

Royal Connections

Grandson: Christian X of Denmark *d. 1947* (❦ page 175)

Married

Louise of the Netherlands *d. 1871*

Children

Louise of Sweden m. Frederick VIII of Denmark *d. 1912* (❦ page 171)

Victor Emmanuel II (1820–78)

KING OF ITALY (1861–78)

House of Savoy

The united kingdom of Italy was established in 1861, after decades of conflict between nations and states, with the former king of Sardinia Victor Emmanuel as its figurehead. He continued to add territories to the new kingdom throughout his reign, including Venetia and, in 1870, the Papal States, after which the capital was established in Rome. The pope's objections to the loss of the Papal States rumbled on until the Lateran Treaty of 1929 formally recognised them as part of Italy in return for the acceptance of Roman Catholicism as the country's religion. Victor Emmanuel married his first cousin Maria Adelaide of Savoy, and their son Umberto inherited the throne on his father's death.

Royal Connections

Grandson: Victor Emmanuel III of Italy *d. 1946* (⚜ page 168)

Married

Maria Adelaide of Austria *d. 1855*

Children

Umberto I of Italy *d. 1900* (⚜ page 159)

Amadeo I of Spain *d. 1890* (⚜ page 156)

Maria Pia m. Louis I of Portugal *d. 1889* (⚜ page 151)

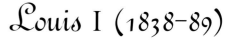

Louis I (1838–89)

KING OF PORTUGAL (1861–89)

House of Braganza-Saxe-Coburg-Gotha

Louis was not unintelligent, but his interests lay in science rather than government, and his reign was marked by stagnation both internationally and domestically. His hesitation meant Portugal lost out on potentially significant territories during the Scramble for Africa in the 1880s, and by the end of his reign the country had fallen far behind others in Europe in terms of technological, social and economic development. The last years of the nineteenth century marked the first steps towards the decline and ultimate fall of the Portuguese monarchy.

Royal Connections

Brothers-in-law: Umberto I of Italy *d. 1900* (⚜ page 159),

Amadeo I of Spain *d. 1890* (⚜ page 156)

Married

Maria Pia of Savoy *d. 1911*

Children

Charles I of Portugal *d. 1908* (⚜ page 163)

William I (1797–1888)

KING OF PRUSSIA (1861–88), GERMAN EMPEROR (1871–88)
House of Hohenzollern

Under William I and his chancellor Otto von Bismarck, Prussia consolidated its position as the leading power among the German states. It was undeniably a two-man achievement – William was a strong figurehead, a good soldier and a talented diplomat, but it was Bismarck who formulated and expedited the policies that led to the establishment of the German Empire. William had never been intended for the throne, but his elder brother's descent into insanity required that William take over government of Prussia as regent in 1858. One of his first acts was to alleviate the strain then existing between the king and the liberal parliament. Conservative by nature, William recognised that, initially at least, he needed parliamentary support. On his full accession in 1861 he began to reveal his own political leanings, and instigated reforms that included an expansion and restructuring of the army and the appointment of Bismarck as chancellor, answerable only to the king. King and minister enjoyed a relationship of mutual respect, if not always accord, although when they disagreed on policy Bismarck usually won the argument. Thus began an era of military conquest that ended, after success in the Franco-Prussian War in 1871, with William being recognised as German Emperor (not Emperor of Germany, which would have implied control of states beyond his hereditary possession). He may have commanded the admiration of his people – and other European powers – but his conservatism and his belief that he had been divinely appointed made him enemies among the liberals. He defied two assassination attempts to die at the age of 90.

Royal Connections
Brother: Frederick William IV of Prussia *d. 1861* (⚜ page 140)

Married
Augusta of Saxe-Weimar *d. 1890*

Children
Frederick III of Germany *d. 1888* (⚜ page 152)

Frederick III (1831–88)

GERMAN EMPEROR (1888)

Frederick, married to Queen Victoria of Great Britain's eldest daughter (also Victoria), was 56 when his father died and he finally came to be German Emperor. By this stage he was suffering cancer of the larynx, and he was destined to play the part he had so long awaited for only 99 days. His son, William II, became the last monarch of the German Empire.

The 'Grandfather of Europe', Christian IX.

Christian IX (1818–1906)

KING OF DENMARK (1863–1906)

House of Schleswig-Holstein-Sonderburg-Glücksburg

The death without heir of Frederick VII caused a war of succession that was eventually won by Christian IX, who had married a cousin of the old king. His predecessor had gained popularity through the abandonment of absolutism and the establishment of a constitutional monarchy. During Christian's reign this constitution was further revised to give parliament greater power.

If Queen Victoria was the grandmother of Europe, Christian was undoubtedly its grandfather. In the early years of the twentieth century, his grandsons sat on the thrones of Denmark, Norway, Greece, Russia and Great Britain by virtue of the dynastic intermarriages of his children, and many of the incumbent monarchs today can claim descent from Christian IX.

Royal Connections

Grandsons: Christian X of Denmark *d. 1947* (page 175),

Haakon VII of Norway *d. 1957* (page 170),

George V of Great Britain and Ireland *d. 1936* (page 174),

Constantine I of Greece *d. 1923* (page 176),

Nicholas II of Russia *d. 1918* (page 165)

Married

Louise of Hesse-Kassel *d. 1898*

Children

Frederick VIII of Denmark *d. 1912* (page 171)

Alexandra m. Edward VII of Great Britain and Ireland *d. 1910* (page 169)

George I of Greece *d. 1913* (page 155)

Dagmar m. Alexander III of Russia *d. 1894* (page 160)

George I (1845–1913)

KING OF GREECE (1863–1913)

House of Schleswig-Holstein-Sonderburg-Glücksburg

The son of the Danish king Christian IX was elected king of Greece by that country's National Assembly after it had forced the abdication of Otto I. Through the marriages of his siblings George found himself allied – in familial terms at least – to the royal houses of Great Britain and Russia, and both powers strongly endorsed his election to the Greek throne. His own marriage, to the niece of Alexander II of Russia, further strengthened the ties.

He was only 17 on his ascension, but was wise enough to realise that the troubles of his predecessor lay largely with his alienation from the Greek people, and George made great efforts to learn the language and traditions of his adopted country. The result was a long reign characterised by territorial expansion and relative stability – despite constant changes in government and occasional dissent between the king and his key ministers. Notable among the lands acquired was Crete, which had long been the subject of campaigns between Greece and the Ottoman Empire.

George died at the hands of an anarchist assassin in March 1913. Partly through personal attitude and partly because of the war that was about to affect every country in Europe, the reigns of his successors proved far more troubled than his own.

George I of Greece had strong family ties with Russia and Britain.

Royal Connections

Father: Christian IX of Denmark *d. 1906* (❧ page 154)

Brothers-in-law: Edward VII of Great Britain and Ireland *d. 1910* (❧ page 169),
Alexander III of Russia *d. 1894* (❧ page 160)

Married

Olga Konstantinova of Russia *d. 1926*

Children

Constantine I of Greece *d. 1923* (❧ page 176)

Amadeo I (1845–90)

KING OF SPAIN (1870–73)

House of Savoy

Amadeo was elected to the Spanish throne by the Cortes after it had deposed Isabella II in 1868. The son of the Italian king Victor Emmanuel II was strongly endorsed by the Spanish general Juan Pim, who was assassinated the same year that Amadeo was sworn in, thus eliminating his most powerful backer. There followed a period of massive internal unrest, in which conspiracies, uprisings and party divides abounded. The army, sent to deal with the uprisings that were breaking out across the country, went on strike and all eyes turned to the king to resolve the problems. Without any kind of support, Amadeo declared the country ungovernable, abdicated and returned to his homeland.

Royal Connections

Brother: Umberto I of Italy *d. 1900* (⚜ page 159)

Brother-in-law: Louis I of Portugal *d. 1889* (⚜ page 151)

Married

Maria Victoria of Cisterna *d. 1876*

Children

Emanuele Filiberto, Duke of Aosta *d. 1931*

Oscar II (1829–1907)

KING OF SWEDEN (1872–1907),

KING OF NORWAY (1872–1905)

House of Bernadotte

Oscar succeeded his brother Charles XV in 1872 and initially refused to grant any concessions towards home rule for Norway. He did, however, make more efforts than his predecessors to be respected by the subjects of his second realm, learning to speak their language fluently. Nevertheless, increasing tension between the king and his Norwegian subjects later resigned him to its inevitable secession and in 1905 he accepted the peaceful dissolution of the union between the two countries. Haakon VII was elected king of the independent Norway.

Oscar was a man of great culture and diplomacy and he was much respected by the rulers of other European powers. In international affairs he preferred a middle ground and maintained neutrality wherever possible. Such was his reputation that he was called upon to arbitrate between other nations on more than one occasion throughout his reign. He was much mourned on his passing in 1907.

Royal Connections

Grandfather: Charles XIV John of Sweden and Norway *d. 1844* (⚜ page 123)

Married

Sophia of Nassau *d. 1913*

Children

Gustav V of Sweden *d. 1950* (⚜ page 173)

Oscar II was renowned across Europe for his even-handedness and sense of justice.

Alfonso may have brought Spain back from the brink of chaos had it not been for his untimely death.

Alfonso XII (1857–85)

KING OF SPAIN (1875–85)

House of Bourbon

Alfonso had gone into exile with his mother when she was deposed in 1868, but he was invited to return and was proclaimed king in 1875. The political turmoil of Amadeo's reign had left the country racked with uncertainty and the restoration of the Bourbon line in Spain was greeted with high hopes for the future. Within a year Alfonso had suppressed the uprisings and agreed to a new constitution that took great strides towards a complete constitutional monarchy. Alfonso did not live to fulfil his potential, dying of tuberculosis before the age of 30.

Royal Connections

Mother: Isabella II of Spain *d. 1904* (✤ page 134)

Married

1. Mercedes of Orléans *d. 1878*
2. Maria Christina of Austria *d. 1929*

Children

Alfonso XIII of Spain *d. 1941* (✤ page 161)

Umberto escaped assassination twice before being shot in 1900.

Umberto I (1844–1900)

KING OF ITALY (1878–1900)
House of Savoy

Victor Emmanuel II's only son Umberto had been brought up with strict military training, and he was much respected as a soldier. A consequence of this early education was that he favoured foreign policy and international affairs over domestic reform. Perhaps the most significant manifestation of this was his agreement to the Triple Alliance with Austria-Hungary and the Prussian-led German states – a pact that held firm into the twentieth century until the First World War.

This policy of allying Italy with its former enemy Austria, combined with Umberto's increasingly conservative attitude – largely manipulated by his wife Margherita of Savoy – brewed resentment in several quarters, most notably among the anarchists. The state of social unrest culminated in the first attempt on Umberto's life in 1878. The anarchist attacker was condemned to death but had his sentence commuted to life by the king. The second attempt was made in 1897 and again the king escaped. Third time proved unlucky, however, as in July 1900 anarchist Gaetano Bresci shot him four times – enough to make sure the conservative king was really dead.

Royal Connections

Brother-in-law: Louis I of Portugal *d. 1889* (♣ page 151)

Brother: Amadeo I of Spain *d. 1873* (♣ page 156)

Married

Margherita of Savoy *d. 1926*

Children

Victor Emmanuel III of Italy *d. 1946* (♣ page 168)

Alexander III was related by marriage to the kings of Greece and Denmark.

Alexander III (1845–94)

TSAR OF RUSSIA (1881–94)

House of Romanov

Believing that his father's assassination had largely been a consequence of his liberal policies, Alexander III set himself a reactionary course that included stricter controls in censorship and education, and a programme of Russification that manifested itself in religious and minority persecution. His reforms were not all detrimental to the stability of Russia, however, and he greatly encouraged industrial development. He died suddenly in 1894, leaving the fate of the Romanovs in the unprepared hands of his son Nicholas.

Royal Connections

Brothers-in-law: George I of Greece *d. 1913* (❦ page 155),
Frederick VIII of Denmark *d. 1912* (❦ page 171)

Married

Dagmar of Denmark *d. 1928*

Children

Nicholas II of Russia *d. 1918* (❦ page 165)

Alfonso XIII was overthrown in favour of the Second Spanish Republic.

Alfonso XIII (1886–1941)

KING OF SPAIN (1886–1931)

House of Bourbon

Alfonso XIII was born three months after the death of his father, in February 1886, and his mother, Maria Christina, was regent until 1902. The 30 or so years of his full reign saw the loss of several Spanish colonies, including Cuba and Puerto Rico, and the rise of dictatorship at the hands of Miguel Primo de Rivera and, later, Francisco Franco.

Alfonso was married to Victoria Eugenie of Battenburg, granddaughter of Queen Victoria and cousin to George V. His mother was an Austrian archduchess. These familial ties laid contradictory claims to loyalty at Alfonso's door during the First World War, but he maintained his country's neutrality throughout. After the war, as a tide of republicanism swept though Europe, Alfonso realised that the monarchy in Spain was falling and in 1931 he resigned the throne without formally abdicating. As king in name only he watched from exile in Fascist Italy as civil war engulfed his kingdom. He abdicated in 1941 in favour of his son Juan Carlos. Franco ruled the Second Spanish Republic from the end of the Civil War, and it was only in 1975 that the monarchy was restored in the form of Alfonso's grandson and the incumbent king of Spain, Juan Carlos I.

Royal Connections

Grandson: Juan Carlos I *b. 1938* (⚜ page 192)

Married

Victoria Eugenie of Battenberg *d. 1969*

Children

Alfonso, Prince of Asturias *d. 1938*

William II (1859–1941)

GERMAN EMPEROR (1888–1918)

House of Hohenzollern

William came to the throne at the age of 29, young and ambitious with visions of a grand expansion of his empire that reflected the divine nature of kingship in which he so strongly believed. Like his grandfather, he recognised that he could not fulfil these ambitions alone, but he could not get along with his grandfather's trusted chancellor Bismarck and within two years the latter had resigned. Successive chancellors wielded great influence over the emperor and shared his expansionist aims.

In the years leading up to the First World War William endeavoured to maintain good relations with Great Britain, but his dreams of an empire to match eventually forced the kingdom of Edward VII into an entente with France. When war finally broke out in 1914 the two grandsons of Queen Victoria found themselves on opposing sides. William's power swiftly declined after this and fell increasingly into the hands of his generals. After Germany's defeat, the US president Woodrow Wilson made it a condition of the peace treaty that William relinquish his rule. By the end of 1918 the emperor had formally abdicated and gone into exile in Holland, where he remained for the rest of his life.

The last monarch of Germany, William II.

Royal Connections

Grandmother: Victoria of Great Britain and Ireland *d. 1901* (⚜ page 137)

Cousin: George V of Great Britain and Ireland *d. 1936* (⚜ page 174)

Married

Augusta Victoria of Schleswig-Holstein *d. 1921*

Children

Crown Prince William *d. 1951*

Charles I (1863–1908)

KING OF PORTUGAL (1889–1908)

House of Braganza-Saxe-Coburg-Gotha

Charles shared his father's lack of aptitude for government but compounded the problem with his narcissistic lifestyle, which resulted in widespread criticism of the monarchy. His personal extravagance and his mismanagement of the country's finances resulted in its bankruptcy on two occasions in the 20 years of his rule and damaged his reputation beyond repair. The king and his eldest son were assassinated in an attack on the royal family as they returned to the palace one day in 1908.

Royal Connections

Uncles: Umberto I of Italy *d. 1900* (⚜ page 159),
Amadeo I of Spain *d. 1890* (⚜ page 156)
Cousin: Victor Emmanuel III of Italy *d. 1946* (⚜ page 168)

Married

Amelia of Orléans *d. 1951*

Children

Manuel II of Portugal *d. 1932* (⚜ page 173)

Charles I and his eldest son were assassinated, leaving the throne to his younger son, Manuel II.

Young Queen Wilhelmina.

Wilhelmina (1880–1962)

QUEEN OF THE NETHERLANDS (1890–1948)

House of Orange-Nassau

Wilhelmina's three older half-brothers predeceased their father William III, leaving his only daughter to inherit the throne, which she did at the age of 10. Her mother, Emma of Waldeck and Pyrmont, acted as regent until Wilhelmina reached 18 and assumed full responsibility.

From the outset Wilhelmina was strong-willed and conservative, but she was tactful enough to accept the limitations of the constitutional monarchy and did not interfere unnecessarily with the government of the country. She ensured that the Netherlands remained strictly neutral throughout the First World War, although the country suffered similar deprivations to many other European nations. She permitted William II of Germany to spend his exile in the Netherlands after the peace of 1918.

The Second World War brought greater hardship for the Dutch people, as Germany invaded in 1940 and occupied the country. Wilhelmina fled to the United Kingdom, where she joined other governments in exile, only returning after the liberation of Holland in 1945. Three years later, after a reign of more than 58 years, she abdicated in favour of her daughter Juliana.

Royal Connections

Great-grandfathers: William I of the Netherlands *d. 1843* (♣ page 120),
Paul I of Russia *d. 1801* (♣ page 107)
Granddaughter: Beatrix of the Netherlands *b. 1938* (♣ page 194)

Married

Hendrik of Mecklenburg-Schwerin *d. 1934*

Children

Juliana of the Netherlands *d. 2004* (♣ page 184)

The last tsar of Russia Nicholas II.

Nicholas II (1868–1918)

TSAR OF RUSSIA (1894–1917)
House of Romanov

Nicholas II was closely related to several other European families in Europe. His mother, Dagmar, was sister to George I of Greece and Frederick VIII of Denmark, and sister-in-law to Edward VII of Britain. Nicholas's own marriage to Alice, Queen Victoria's granddaughter (known as Alexandra after her introduction to the Russian royal family), tied him more closely to Britain.

Nicholas was well-intentioned but singularly unsuited to ruling a country in political and civil turmoil. He resisted moves towards democracy, believing that autocratic rule worked to everyone's greatest benefit, but defeat in the First World War plunged Russia into revolution. Forced to abdicate in 1917, the tsar was placed under house arrest. Transferred to Ekaterinburg in the Urals, on 17 July the following year Nicholas II, his wife and his five children were taken into the cellars of their house and executed. The longest uninterrupted dynasty in early modern European history was laid to rest in an instant.

Royal Connections

Cousins: George V of Great Britain and Ireland *d. 1936* (❧ page 174),

Haakon VII of Norway *d. 1957* (❧ page 170),

Constantine I of Greece *d. 1923* (❧ page 176),

Christian X of Denmark *d. 1947* (❧ page 175)

Married

Alice of Great Britain *d. 1918*

Children

Tsarevich Alexei *d. 1918*

1900-Present

From the House of Saxe-Coburg-Gotha to the House of Windsor

Edward VII to Elizabeth II

Victor Emmanuel III's reign represented the last gasp of the monarchy in Italy.

his concord with Austria-Hungary and Germany through the Triple Alliance. Ultimately he threw in his lot with the Allies.

The interwar years in Italy brought Benito Mussolini and his Fascists to power, and reduced the king to a nominal ruler, but he supported Mussolini's early involvement in the Second World War. Increasing dissatisfaction with Italy's losses, however, led him to arrest Mussolini in 1943. It proved too late to win favour, and the following year, in an attempt to preserve the monarchy, he passed the royal prerogative to his son Umberto. Two years later he officially abdicated, and his son ruled briefly as the last king of Italy.

Royal Connections
Uncles: Louis I of Portugal *d. 1889* (⚜ page 151),
Amadeo I of Spain *d. 1873* (⚜ page 156)

Married
Elena of Montenegro *d. 1952*

Children
Umberto II of Italy *d. 1983* (⚜ page 168)

Victor Emmanuel III (1869–1947)

KING OF ITALY (1900–46)
House of Savoy

Victor Emmanuel III's reign spanned the most turbulent period in modern European history and ended in the fall of the Italian monarchy. He acceded to the throne on the assassination of his father Umberto I and was thrown immediately into war with Turkey. As the decade progressed and war in Europe became increasingly likely, the king tried to maintain neutrality despite

Umberto II (1904–83)

KING OF ITALY (1946)
When his father Victor Emmanuel III abdicated in 1946, Umberto officially became king of Italy. It was an empty title. A month later, in the wake of the Second World War, the Republic of Italy was declared and Umberto and his father spent the rest of their lives in exile.

Edward VII (1841–1910)

KING OF GREAT BRITAIN AND IRELAND (1901–10)
House of Saxe-Coburg-Gotha

Edward was nearly 60 years old when he inherited the British throne from his mother Queen Victoria. By this time the pleasures of his youth had taken their toll and he had little to offer the country except a passion for monarchical ceremony.

Victoria had loved but mistrusted her eldest son and was disappointed by the scandal that he left in his wake throughout his youth. In an effort to tame his wild side he was married off to the princess of Denmark in 1863 and the couple had five children, including the future George V. The alliance of Britain and Denmark caused concern in some quarters, as Denmark and Germany were in dispute over the provinces of Schleswig and Holstein, and Victoria's German ties were strong. Edward was never faithful to his wife and entertained several mistresses, including the actress Lillie Langtry and Jennie Jerome, mother of Winston Churchill.

With little interest in politics Edward relied on his charm and good nature to earn the love of his subjects, and succeeded in doing so despite his practical shortcomings. He was mourned on his death as a man who had never been given the chance to prove his worth. His great-grandson is the incumbent king of Norway, Harald V, and his great-granddaughter is Elizabeth II of Britain.

The only British king of the House of Saxe-Coburg-Gotha, Edward VII.

Royal Connections

Father-in-law: Christian IX of Denmark *d. 1906* (⚜ page 154)

Nephew: William II of Germany *d. 1941* (⚜ page 162)

Grandsons: Edward VIII of Great Britain and Ireland *d. 1972* (⚜ page 180),

George VI of Great Britain and Ireland *d. 1952* (⚜ page 181),

Olav V of Norway *d. 1991* (⚜ page 187),

Married

Alexandra of Denmark *d. 1925*

Children

George V of Great Britain and Ireland *d. 1936* (⚜ page 174)

Maud m. Haakon VII of Norway *d. 1957* (⚜ page 170)

Haakon VII (1872–1957)

KING OF NORWAY (1905–57)
House of Glücksburg-Oldenburg

Haakon's ancestry combined bloodlines from the other northern kingdoms Sweden and Denmark.

For centuries Norway had been ruled by one or other of its two powerful neighbours and control of the country had passed between Sweden and Denmark. When Norway peacefully dissolved the union with Sweden in 1905, Haakon was elected king of the newly independent country. His father was the Danish king Frederick VIII and his mother the only daughter of Charles XV of Sweden. Through his father's siblings he also numbered the rulers of Britain, Russia and Greece among his first cousins, and he cemented ties with Britain by marrying his cousin Maud, daughter of Edward VII.

Haakon was a strong ruler through the difficult years of both World Wars and earned particular admiration for his courageous stand against German demands when troops occupied Norway in 1940. For almost the entirety of the Second World War Haakon was forced to run his government in exile from England. The loyalty of the Norwegian people to their king and country never failed and Haakon was welcomed home with great emotion after the war. His popularity endured until his death in 1957.

Royal Connections

Father-in-law: Edward VII of Great Britain and Ireland *d. 1910* (❧ page 169)

Brother: Christian X of Denmark *d. 1947* (❧ page 175)

Cousins: George V of Great Britain and Ireland *d. 1936* (❧ page 174),

Nicholas II of Russia *d. 1918* (❧ page 165),

Constantine I of Greece *d. 1923* (❧ page 176)

Married

Maud of Wales *d. 1938*

Children

Olav V of Norway *d. 1991* (❧ page 187)

Frederick VIII (1843–1912)

KING OF DENMARK (1906–12)

House of Schleswig-Holstein-Sonderburg-Glücksburg

Frederick's son Haakon was already king of Norway when he acceded to the Danish throne in 1906. His age and ill-health meant he had only a few years to make his mark on the history of Denmark. He was a renowned soldier, participating in the unsuccessful war of 1864 to retain Schleswig-Holstein, and had a keen interest in military policy throughout his life. The current king of Norway is his great-grandson and the queen of Denmark his great-granddaughter. He is also related to the ruling families of Belgium and Luxembourg through his daughter Ingeborg.

Royal Connections

Father-in-law: Charles XV of Sweden and Norway *d. 1872* (⚜ page 148)

Nephews: George V of Great Britain and Ireland *d. 1936* (⚜ page 174),

Nicholas II of Russia *d. 1918* (⚜ page 165),

Constantine I of Greece *d. 1923* (⚜ page 176)

Grandsons: Frederick IX of Denmark *d. 1972* (⚜ page 183),

Olav V of Norway *d. 1991* (⚜ page 187)

Married

Louisa of Sweden *d. 1926*

Children

Christian X of Denmark *d. 1947* (⚜ page 175)

Haakon VII of Norway *d. 1957* (⚜ page 170)

Frederick VIII's descendants today sit on the thrones of Norway, Denmark, Belgium and Luxembourg.

During the Second World War, Gustav's loyalties were questioned because of his heritage, but he remained neutral throughout.

Gustav V (1858–1950)

KING OF SWEDEN (1907–50)

House of Bernadotte

Trained in the army, Gustav retained a lifelong interest in military affairs and held the position of commander-in-chief of the armed forces for more than 20 years from the start of his reign. This spanned the period of both World Wars, and Gustav's loyalties came under scrutiny during both events. His wife was a granddaughter of William I of Germany, and the king is known to have had friends among those who later became Nazi leaders. However, he adopted a policy of neutrality that endured through both wars. His reputation declined after his death when allegations of his bisexuality were made by a man claiming to have been Gustav's lover. He was succeeded by his son Gustav VI Adolf.

Royal Connections

Uncle: Charles XV of Sweden and Norway

d. 1872 (❀ page 148)

Married

Victoria of Baden *d. 1930*

Children

Gustav VI Adolf of Sweden *d. 1973* (❀ page 185)

Manuel II – Portugal's last king.

Manuel II (1889–1932)

KING OF PORTUGAL (1908–10)

House of Braganza-Saxe-Corbug-Gotha

By the time Manuel came to the Portuguese throne on the assassination of his father and elder brother in 1908 it was clear that days of the monarchy were numbered. In an effort to regain some popularity he declared open elections, but the plan backfired and the republicans won a landslide victory. As revolution swept the country in 1910 Manuel sought a safe haven in Britain, and despite plans to reinstate the Braganzas on the throne of Portugal, royalty in the country had reached the point of no return. The last king of Portugal died, still in exile, in 1932.

Royal Connections

Great-grandfather: Victor Emmanuel II of Italy

d. 1878 (❀ page 151)

Married

Augusta Victoria of Hohenzollern-Sigmaringen

d. 1966

Children

None

George V's reign saw his extended family pitted against one another in the First World War.

George V (1865–1936)

KING OF GREAT BRITAIN AND IRELAND (1910–36)

House of Windsor

A faithful husband and loving father (although he continued the tradition of royal Georges by falling out with his eldest son), devoted to his subjects and with a strong sense of his responsibilities as monarch, George V could not have been more different from his father. As a second son, he had not been groomed for kingship and this perhaps gave him the simple and genuine air that made him so beloved. He was thrust into the limelight in 1892 when his elder brother Albert died, leaving him second in line to his grandmother's throne.

The dominant event of his reign was the First World War. It was a time of personal disquiet for George V. Britain was ranged against the Germany of his cousin Kaiser William II, who was forced to abdicate as part of the peace agreement in 1918. Even the German name of the king's own family was changed to Windsor. The last year of the war also saw the fall of the Russian monarchy with the execution of another cousin, Nicholas II. Sensing his impending doom, the Russian tsar had applied to his cousin in England for sanctuary, but the political climate of the time forced the king to refuse – effectively sealing the fate of the Russian royal family. Monarchies across Europe fell as boundaries were redrawn, but the British monarchy survived the war intact. George V died, however, worrying that his wayward son might yet bring it to destruction.

Royal Connections

Cousins: William II of Germany *d. 1941* (❦ page 162),
Nicholas II of Russia *d. 1918* (❦ page 165)

Married

Mary of Teck *d. 1953*

Children

Edward VIII of Great Britain and Ireland *d. 1972* (❦ page 180)

George VI of Great Britain and Ireland *d. 1936* (❦ page 181)

Christian X (1870–1947)

KING OF DENMARK (1912–47)

House of Schleswig-Holstein-Sonderburg-Glücksburg

Christian encapsulated all that a modern monarchy should have represented in the troubled early years of the twentieth century. His policies were progressive, including the granting of equal suffrage to men and women. Despite pressure from Germany he maintained Denmark's neutrality throughout the First World War.

He is best remembered for his courage in the face of Nazi occupation of his country. After the invasion in 1940 the king would be seen parading through the streets, defying his enemies and showing that he would never relinquish his sovereignty. His public presence kept up the morale of the Danish people and his message of freedom hung in the air even when he was placed under house arrest in 1943. He emerged from the war a popular symbol of national resistance. He died two years later, having outlived his many royal cousins.

Royal Connections

Nephew: Olav V of Norway *d. 1991* (❦ page 187)

Cousins: George V of Great Britain and Ireland *d. 1936* (❦ page 174),

Nicholas II of Russia *d. 1918* (❦ page 165),

Constantine I of Greece *d. 1923* (❦ page 176)

Granddaughter: Margrethe II of Denmark *b. 1940* (❦ page 189)

Married

Alexandrine of Mecklenburg-Schwerin *d. 1952*

Children

Frederick IX of Denmark *d. 1972* (❦ page 183)

The disagreements between Constantine and his government over loyalties during the First World War ultimately led to his abdication.

Constantine I (1868–1923)

KING OF GREECE (1913–17, 1920–22)
House of Schleswig-Holstein-Sonderburg-Glücksburg

Constantine succeeded to the throne of Greece after the assassination of his father at the hands of an anarchist in 1913, on the eve of the Great War. He had received military training in Prussia and was married to the sister of Kaiser William of Germany; his loyalties thus lay with the Central Powers when the war broke out. His government, however, was keen to ally Greece with the Entente countries and this led to the dismissal of the prime minister Venizelos in favour of a series of premiers more in sympathy with Constantine. But the Greek army was persuaded to defy the king and join the fight against Germany. Unable to resist the threat of arms, Constantine abdicated in 1917. His second son Alexander took his place briefly, but Constantine was reinstated in 1920. He never fully regained his popularity, however, and abdicated once again in 1922, dying the following year.

Royal Connections

Brother-in-law: William II of Germany *d. 1941* (page 162)

Cousins: Christian X of Denmark *d. 1947* (page 175),

Haakon VII of Norway *d. 1957* (page 170),

George V of Great Britain and Ireland *d. 1936* (page 174),

Nicholas II of Russia *d. 1918* (page 165)

Married

Sophie of Prussia *d. 1932*

Children

George II of Greece *d. 1947* (page 179)

Alexander of Greece *d. 1920* (page 178)

Charles I (1887–1922)

EMPEROR OF AUSTRIA (1916–18),

KING OF HUNGARY (1916–18)

House of Habsburg

The assassination of Archduke Francis Ferdinand had triggered the First World War and left succession to the throne of Austria-Hungary open to his son Charles. In the turmoil of war there was little he could do to reverse the empire's fortunes. Towards the end of 1918 he attempted to save the monarchy by declaring Austria a federative state, but Hungary had insisted on its independence and Charles had no choice but to sign an unconditional surrender to the Allies.

A devout Catholic, Charles died in exile in 1922, never having formally abdicated the thrones. His son Otto is the current head of the Habsburg house and pretender to the thrones of Austria and Hungary.

Royal Connections

Great-grandmother: Maria II of Portugal *d. 1853* (♣ page 127)

Married

Zita of Bourbon-Parma *d. 1989*

Children

Crown Prince Otto *b. 1912*

The last of Austria's Habsburg rulers, Charles I.

Alexander was interim king of Greece during his father's enforced periods of exile.

Alexander (1893–1920)

KING OF GREECE (1917–20)

House of Schleswig-Holstein-Sonderburg-Glücksburg

Alexander held the throne of Greece for three years between the two periods of his father's rule. Constantine was expelled during the First World War because of his pro-German sympathies, as was his eldest son George. Alexander was considered a better choice as his loyalties were less fixed. He shocked the establishment by marrying a commoner, Aspasia Manos, when plans were afoot for a union with George V of Britain's daughter Mary. He died after contracting septicaemia from a monkey bite. His daughter Alexandra, born after his death, married the Yugoslav king Peter II.

Royal Connections

Brother: George II of Greece *d. 1947* (⚜ page 179)

Married

Aspasia Manos *d. 1972*

Children

Alexandra *d. 1993*

George II (1890-1947)

KING OF GREECE (1922–24, 1935–47)

House of Schleswig-Holstein-Sonderburg-Glücksburg

The eldest son of Constantine I went with his father into exile in 1917 and watched as his younger brother wore the crown of Greece for three years. On the reinstatement of Constantine in 1920 George once again became heir apparent, and succeeded to the throne on his father's final abdication in 1922. His first tenure as king was brief – he was asked to leave the country while the National Assembly considered how it should be run. Its conclusion favoured a republic and George was deposed in 1924. For more than 10 years he travelled around Europe, eventually settling in England in 1932 from where he was recalled to Greece three years later after a government overthrow and massive vote in favour of the restoration of the monarchy.

As the Second World War swept across Europe George made clear his pro-British sympathies, and German occupation in Greece forced him back to England to run his government in exile. His return after the war was met with mixed feelings in Greece, although the monarchists won the majority in the 1946 elections. George died the following year, leaving the realm to his brother Paul.

Royal Connections

Great-grandfather: Christian IX of Denmark *d. 1906* (❧ page 154)

Brothers: Alexander of Greece *d. 1920* (❧ page 178),

Paul I of Greece *d. 1964* (❧ page 182)

Married

Elisabeth of Romania *d. 1956*

Children

None

George II was exiled with his father during the First World War.

Edward VIII was created Duke of Windsor after his abdication, and lived the rest of his life abroad.

Edward VIII (1894–1972)

KING OF GREAT BRITAIN AND IRELAND (1936)
House of Windsor

In his youth the eldest son of George V seemed more like his grandfather than his father, enjoying royal ceremony and with ample natural charm. His headstrong nature was demonstrated by his refusal to sacrifice the woman he loved – the twice-divorced American Wallis Simpson – for the throne. He reigned for just 11 months, during which time a political consensus emerged that Simpson was not acceptable as queen. In a moving speech Edward abdicated in December 1936, and the crown passed to his ill-prepared but ultimately more suitable brother, George VI.

Royal Connections

Niece: Elizabeth II of Great Britain and Ireland *b. 1926* (⚜ page 186)

Cousin: Olav V of Norway *d. 1991* (⚜ page 187)

Married

Wallis Simpson *d. 1986*

Children

None

George VI (1895–1952)

KING OF GREAT BRITAIN (1936–52)

House of Windsor

The 'Year of Three Kings' in Britain concluded with the accession of George VI in December 1936. The unprepared Duke of York had barely come to terms with the idea before he was forced to assume the responsibilities of the throne. He was by nature a shy man who stammered when he spoke, and the thought of his new royal duties was said to have terrified him. He was helped through this difficult time – and those that followed – by his wife Elizabeth, later Queen Elizabeth the Queen Mother. Her devotion to her husband, her children and the country of which she had so suddenly become queen consort were exemplary, and continued to be so until her death in 2002 nearly 50 years after that of her husband.

For almost half George V's reign Britain was at war, and through this time the king and queen proved ideal figureheads for a nation in crisis. When bombs began dropping on London in 1940 they refused to leave Buckingham Palace, preferring to share the trials of their subjects rather than escape them. The war inaugurated the final decline of Britain as a global power and by the end of George's reign the once-great empire was rapidly shrinking.

George VI restored the popularity of the monarchy in Britain after the abdication crisis.

Royal Connections

Cousin: Olav V of Norway *d. 1991* (❧ page 187)

Married

Elizabeth Bowes-Lyon *d. 2002*

Children

Elizabeth II of Great Britain *b. 1926*

Paul of Greece, with his wife Frederika and their children.

Paul (1901–1964)

KING OF GREECE (1947–64)

House of Schleswig-Holstein-Sonderburg-Glücksburg

Paul was the third of Constantine I's sons to wear the Greek crown. He was exiled with his father and eldest brother George after Constantine was deposed in 1917, and during the Second World War he lived in England with the government in exile.

George II died in the midst of the civil war that was raging between the government and the communists, which followed the defeat of the occupying powers, and Paul thus inherited a fragile kingdom. Within two years the Communists had been restrained but the country, particularly the north, had been reduced to ruins. For the rest of his reign Paul worked hard to stabilise Greece domestically, economically and with regards international affairs. The latter took him abroad frequently and his long periods of absence were noted with dissatisfaction by groups already leaning towards republicanism. He died from stomach cancer in 1964. Unlike his two brothers, Paul at last produced an heir, who became the last king of Greece.

Royal Connections

Great-grandfather: Christian IX of Denmark *d. 1906* (♣ page 154)

Brothers: Alexander of Greece *d. 1920* (♣ page 178),

George II of Greece *d. 1947* (♣ page 179)

Married

Frederika of Hanover *d. 1981*

Children

Constantine II of Greece *b. 1940* (♣ page 188)

Sophia m. Juan Carlos I of Spain *b. 1938* (♣ page 192)

Frederick IX (1899–1972)

KING OF DENMARK (1947–72)

House of Schleswig-Holstein-Sonderburg-Glücksburg

F rederick was raised in the military tradition, but broke the habit of his forebears by going into the navy rather than the army. He came to the throne in the wake of the Second World War, during which his father had become much beloved as a symbol of Danish strength and resistance to foreign threat. Frederick sought to maintain this reputation with his democratic style.

With the thrones of Denmark and Norway already allied through the blood of his grandfather, Frederick strengthened ties with the third Nordic kingdom by marrying the daughter of the heir to the Swedish throne in 1935. The couple had three daughters but no sons, so the king amended the constitution to allow for his eldest child, Margrethe, to inherit the throne on his death. She is the current ruling monarch of Denmark.

Royal Connections

Father-in-law: Gustav VI Adolf of Sweden *d. 1973* (⚜ page 185)

Cousin: Olav V of Norway *d. 1991* (⚜ page 187)

Married

Ingrid of Sweden *d. 2000*

Children

Margrethe II of Denmark *b. 1940* (⚜ page 189)

Anne-Marie m. Constantine II of Greece *b. 1940* (⚜ page 188)

Frederick IX, father to the incumbent Danish queen.

Following in the tradition of her mother, Juliana abdicated in favour of her daughter in 1980.

Juliana (1909–2004)

QUEEN OF THE NETHERLANDS (1948–80)

House of Orange-Nassau

Juliana became queen of the Netherlands on her mother's abdication in 1948, although she had been acting as regent for several months during Wilhelmina's last illness. Her education had been geared towards her eventual succession, and although she was a shy young woman she was well prepared to assume royal responsibilities when the time came.

Her marriage in 1936 to a German prince was taken by Hitler to suggest an alliance between Holland and Germany, but Queen Wilhelmina swiftly crushed the suggestion and the Netherlands found itself on the receiving end of Nazi occupation throughout the Second World War. Juliana spent this time in exile with her family.

After her accession she fell under the influence of a faith healer whom she had asked to help her blind daughter Christina, and rumours of an affair began to chip away at her popularity. As time passed, however, the public began to see her as a modern and accessible monarch in touch with her subjects, and she retained her popularity for the rest of her reign.

Juliana abdicated in 1980 in favour of her daughter Beatrix, the incumbent queen of the Netherlands.

Royal Connections

Mother: Wilhelmina of the Netherlands *d. 1962* (✤ page 164)

Married

Bernhard of Lippe-Biesterfeld *d. 2004*

Children

Beatrix of the Netherlands *b. 1938* (✤ page 194)

Gustav VI Adolf (1882–1973)

KING OF SWEDEN (1950–73)

House of Bernadotte

Gustav VI Adolf was 67 years old when he came to the throne, and he completed the work begun by his father of amending the constitution to moderate the influence of the monarchy. Affable and capable, he grew to be much respected by his subjects and turned the tide of anti-monarchist feeling in Sweden.

His cultural interests were broad. He was a keen botanist, for which he was admitted to the British Royal Society, and he enjoyed travelling abroad on archeological digs. His first wife was a granddaughter of Queen Victoria (by her third son Arthur and his wife Louisa Margaret of Prussia) and his second, Louise Mountbatten, was also loosely related to the British royal family. He outlived his son and heir, so on his death the throne passed to his grandson Carl XVI Gustav.

Royal Connections

Grandchildren: Margrethe of Denmark *b. 1940* (❀ page 189),

Carl XVI Gustav of Sweden *b. 1946* (❀ page 190)

Married

1. Margaret of Connaught *d. 1920*

2. Louise Mountbatten *d. 1965*

Children

Gustav Adolf, Duke of Västerbotten *d. 1947*

Ingrid m. Frederick IX of Denmark *d. 1972* (❀ page 183)

Gustav VI Adolf restored the popularity of the monarchy in Sweden, which had been in decline since the end of the war.

Elizabeth II (b. 1926)

QUEEN OF GREAT BRITAIN (1952–PRESENT)

House of Windsor

Like her father, Elizabeth II demonstrated a devotion to her country and a love of family life that endeared her to the people of Britain even before she succeeded the throne. The early death of George VI led to her assuming responsibility at a relatively young age, but throughout her long and often difficult reign she has maintained her dignity and dedication.

During Elizabeth's reign the last remnants of Britain's empire were relinquished.

Her years as queen have been characterised by personal misfortune, largely through the marital problems of her children, three of whom are divorced, including the heir apparent Charles, Prince of Wales. She also came under early criticism for being perceived as unapproachable and out of touch with the common people. Her great efforts to rectify this image – through allowing unprecedented media access to her life and family – were successful and although she retains a royal reserve, her subjects have developed a fondness for the royal family that has endured crises such as the monarch's reaction to the death of Diana, Princess of Wales.

In recent years the British monarchy has experienced a revival of popularity, both national and international, which was evidenced by the public displays of affection at the queen's eightieth birthday celebrations in 2006. There is no tradition of abdication in the United Kingdom and Elizabeth has stated that she intends to rule for as long as she is able.

Royal Connections

Grandfather: George V of Great Britain and Ireland *d. 1936* (⚜ page 174)

Uncle: Edward VIII of Great Britain and Ireland *d. 1972* (⚜ page 180)

Married

Philip of Denmark and Greece *b. 1921*

Children

Charles, Prince of Wales *b. 1948*

Anne, Princess Royal *b. 1950*

Andrew, Duke of York *b. 1960*

Edward, Earl of Wessex *b. 1964*

Olav V (1903–91)

KING OF NORWAY (1957–91)

House of Glücksberg-Oldenburg

During the Second World War Olav initially joined his family in exile. In 1944 he was given command of the Norwegian armed forces and played an active part in the struggle to liberate Norway and return to his realm. He returned, along with the rest of the royal family, in 1945.

His stalwart defence of Norway during the Second World War had already gained him popularity, and he built on this after his accession to the throne in 1957, earning himself the nickname the 'People's King'. He continued his role as commander-in-chief and took his responsibilities towards the army as seriously as he did those towards his subjects. His death in 1991 provoked unprecedented public mourning.

Royal Connections

Grandfather: Edward VII of Great Britain and Ireland
d. 1910 (⚜ page 169)
Cousin: Frederick IX of Denmark *d. 1972* (⚜ page 183)

Married

Martha of Sweden *d. 1954*

Children

Harald V of Norway *b. 1937* (⚜ page 195)

The 'People's King', Olav V.

Constantine II has lived in exile since he was deposed in 1973.

Constantine II (b. 1940)

KING OF GREECE (1964–73)

House of Schleswig-Holstein-Sonderburg-Glücksburg

The last king of Greece spent his early years with his family in exile abroad, during his country's occupation by the Germans. He showed early promise as an athlete and won a gold medal for sailing at the 1960 Rome Olympics. Four years later, just before his accession to the throne, he married the Danish princess Anne-Marie.

The prime minister, George Papandreou, was a republican but initially at least the premier and the king made efforts to reconcile their different philosophies. Their relationship quickly deteriorated, however, and the prime minister was dismissed after a scandal involving his son. Constantine's search for a more royalist replacement caused civil strife and by 1967 the army had seized power. The king and his family were exiled in Rome. From this time he was king in name only and in 1973 a plebiscite voted in favour of the Greek republic. Today, stripped of his status even as a Greek citizen, he resides in England.

Royal Connections

Uncles: Alexander of Greece *d. 1920* (page 178),
George II of Greece *d. 1947* (page 179)
Sister-in-law: Margrethe II of Denmark *b. 1940* (page 189)
Brother-in-law: Juan Carlos I of Spain *b. 1938* (page 192)

Married

Anne-Marie of Denmark *b. 1946*

Children

Princess Alexia *b. 1965*   Crown Prince Pavlos *b. 1967*

Price Nikolaos *b. 1969*   Princess Theodora *b. 1983*

Prince Philippos *b. 1986*

Margrethe II (b. 1940)

QUEEN OF DENMARK (1972–PRESENT)

House of Schleswig-Holstein-Sonderburg-Glücksburg

When it became clear that Frederick IX was not going to produce a male heir, it was assumed that his younger brother Knud would inherit the throne, according to existing Danish law. However, the old king amended the constitution and bestowed the right of succession on his eldest daughter and her heirs. Margrethe therefore came to the throne when her father died, after a brief illness, in 1972.

In the tradition of her grandfather and father, Margrethe is considered one of the most progressive and accessible of the modern European monarchs. She takes an active and public role in Danish life, hosting and attending many events and is an advocate of political and religious tolerance. Although Denmark is a constitutional monarchy, and the queen cannot make political decisions independent of parliament, she maintains a keen interest and participation in affairs of state representation of the Danish monarchy abroad.

Margrethe's sister Anne-Marie married the king of Greece, Constantine II, in 1964 and was queen regnant until the Greek monarchy was dissolved in 1973. Margrethe herself married the French diplomat Henry de Laborde de Monpezat in 1967, and the birth of two sons by the end of the decade ensured the future of the Danish monarchy.

Royal Connections

Cousin: Carl XVI Gustav of Sweden *b. 1946* (❧ page 190)

Brother-in-law: Constantine II of Greece *b. 1940* (❧ page 188)

Married

Henry de Laborde de Monpezat *b. 1934*

Children

Crown Prince Frederick *b. 1968*

Prince Joachim *b. 1969*

Carl XVI Gustav (b. 1946)

KING OF SWEDEN (1973–PRESENT)

House of Bernadotte

The current king of Sweden became second in line to the throne when he was only a few months old, on the death of his father in 1947. Three years later, on the death of his great-grandfather, he became heir apparent. After school he followed the royal tradition of training in the armed forces and received commissions in army, navy and air force. He was also taught the finer points of government in preparation for his accession to the throne in 1973.

Limited by the Swedish constitution to ceremonial duties and those as representative of his country, Carl XVI Gustav has proved himself an able ambassador. He is passionate about environmental issues and has broad personal interests, including cars and scouting. It is he who presides over the annual Nobel Prize ceremony in Stockholm.

Royal Connections

Cousin: Margrethe II of Denmark *b. 1940* (❧ page 189)

Married

Silvia Sommerlath *b. 1943*

Children

Crown Princess Victoria *b. 1977*

Carl Philip, Duke of Värmland *b. 1979*

Madeleine, Duchess of Hälsingland and Gästrikland *b. 1982*

Carl XVI Gustav, with his wife Silvia and their three children, Carl Philip, Victoria and Madeleine.

Juan Carlos I (b. 1938)

KING OF SPAIN (1975–PRESENT)

House of Bourbon

After the abdication of Alfonso XIII the exiled Spanish royal family settled in Italy. Alfonso's son and rightful heir to the Spanish throne, Juan of Bourbon, fought strongly against the republic and the dictatorship of Francisco Franco. Franco himself declared that on his death control of the country should fall into the hands not of Juan but of his son Juan Carlos, returning Spain to the monarchy, albeit under a strict constitution. Franco himself oversaw the young Juan Carlos's education, ensuring he was well trained in the military arts and the procedures of government.

In 1962, the Spanish heir married the daughter of the Greek king Paul I and consolidated the Bourbon line with the birth of two daughters and a son within six years. In 1975, two days after Franco's death, he was formally proclaimed king and began the process of democratising his country. Although this caused friction with Francoist and conservative elements, initially Juan Carlos avoided alienating these factions. As his reign progressed, however, and the new constitution was implemented, he faced a military coup in 1981 in which armed forces stormed the Cortes, in the process of electing a new prime minister, and attempted a more authoritarian monarchy. Juan Carlos's refusal to have any part in the coup ensured its failure. Today, under Juan Carlos, Spain remains a democracy.

Royal Connections

Father-in-law: Paul I of Greece *d. 1964* (❀ page 182)

Married

Sophia of Greece and Denmark *b. 1938*

Children

Elena, Duchess of Lugo *b. 1963*

Cristina, Duchess of Palma de Mallorca *b. 1965*

Felipe, Prince of Asturias *b. 1968*

Beatrix (b. 1938)

QUEEN OF THE NETHERLANDS (1980–PRESENT)

House of Orange-Nassau

The third successive female monarch of the Netherlands, Beatrix came to the throne on the abdication of her 71-year-old mother in 1980. Her education began in Canada when the family were exiled there during the Second World War and continued after their return to the Netherlands in 1945. Her mother installed her on the Council of State on her eighteenth birthday, the date at which she could legally inherit the throne in her own right.

Beatrix courted controversy in 1965 by announcing her engagement to the German Claus von Amsberg. Her fiancé had been a member of the Hitler Youth and the German army, and these facts alone caused an outcry. Beatrix weathered the storm, however, and her husband did much to endear himself to the Dutch people throughout his life. The couple had three sons, promising at last a male succession in the Netherlands.

She remains a popular queen, having overcome questions at the beginning of her reign about the long-term future of the monarchy. Although her input in government affairs is limited constitutionally she wields more control in international affairs, and has been known to insist on having her way in such matters despite objections from internal parties. Recently there has been speculation about whether she will follow the pattern of her mother and grandmother, and abdicate in favour of her eldest son. Beatrix herself has given no indication of whether or not she will do so.

Queen Beatrix plays an active role in the government of the Netherlands.

Royal Connections

Grandmother: Wilhelmina of the Netherlands *d. 1962* (❧ page 164)

Married

Claus von Amsberg *d. 2002*

Children

Willem-Alexander, Prince of Orange *b. 1967*

Prince Johan-Friso *b. 1968*

Prince Constantijn *b. 1969*

Harald V (b. 1937)

KING OF NORWAY (1991–PRESENT)

House of Glücksburg-Oldenburg

Harald spent his early years in exile in the United States throughout the Second World War, while his father conducted a government in exile in England, but the family returned to Norway in 1945. He was inducted into the Council of State when he was 20 and from that time he played a role in official royal duties, acting as regent whenever his father was away.

His marriage in 1968 to a commoner, Sonja Haraldson, caused some controversy, but this soon passed and Harald's popularity revitalised. Like his father, Harald was a keen sportsman, and has represented his country at sailing in the Olympic Games.

In recent years Harald has reduced his royal duties on the grounds of ill-health, and his son and heir, Crown Prince Haakon has assumed a more prominent role in state affairs.

Royal Connections

Grandfather: Haakon VII of Norway *d. 1957* (❧ page 170)

Great-uncle: Christian X of Denmark *d. 1947* (❧ page 175)

Married

Sonja Haraldson *b. 1937*

Children

Princess Martha Louise *b. 1971*

Crown Prince Haakon *b. 1973*

Harald V has recently taken a less prominent role in government, passing the reins to his son Haakon.

Rulers by Region

Picture Credits

1 Joseph Stieler (1799–1856), *A Portrait of King Oscar of Sweden as Crown Prince*, 1823, courtesy of akg images © Sotheby's

3 George Hayter (1792–1871), *Queen Victoria*, 1863, courtesy of the National Portrait Gallery, London

4 Carlo Maratti, after Van Dyck (1625–1713), *Charles I in Three Positions*, courtesy of Bridgeman Art Library © The Trustees of the Weston Park Foundation, UK

5 artist unknown, *King Gustav V Adolph of Sweden*, courtesy of The Art Archive/Gripsholm Castle, Sweden/Dagli Orti

6 Antoine-Francois Callet (18th century), *Portrait of Louis XVI*, 1788, courtesy of Corbis © Johansen Krause/Archivo Iconografico, S.A.

7 Elisabeth Vigée-Lebrun (1755–1842), *Stanislas II Auguste Poniatowski*, 1802, courtesy of Topham Picturepoint/Roger-Viollet

8–9 Louis de Silvestre (1675–1760), *Frederick Augustus II*, courtesy of Bridgeman Art Library/Gemaeldegalerie Alte Meister, Dresden, Germany © Staatliche Kunstsammlungen Dresden

10 Austrian School (17th century), *Portrait of Sigismund III*, courtesy of Bridgeman Art Library © Royal Castle, Warsaw, Poland/Maciej Bronarski

11 artist unknown, *Christian IV of Denmark*, courtesy of Topham Picturepoint

12 Antoine-Françis Sergent-Marceau (1751–1847), *Henry IV, King of France and Navarre*, *c.*1787–91, courtesy of Corbis © Stapleton Collection

13 artist unknown, *Henry IV of France*, courtesy of Topham Picturepoint/HIP

14 Diego Velázquez (1599–1660), *Philip III on Horseback*, 1631–36, courtesy of Corbis © Archivo Iconografico, S.A.

15 John de Critz the Elder (17th century), *The Sutherland Portrait of James VI Scotland*, *c.* 1600–25, courtesy of Corbis © Fine Art Photographic Library

16 Philippe de Champaigne (1602–74), *Louis XIII of France*, *c.* 1640, courtesy of akg images/Erich Lessing

17 artist unknown, *Gustav II Adolf of Sweden*, courtesy of The Art Archive/Kalmar Castle, Sweden/Dagli Orti

18 Lucas van Valckenborch (1535–97), *Portrait of the Archduke Matthias as P. Cornelius Scipio Maior*, 1580, courtesy of akg images/Erich Lessing

19 Grigoriy Ivanovich Ugryumov (1764–1823), *The Election of the Tsar Michael Romanov*, courtesy of Bridgeman Art Library/Tretyakov Gallery, Moscow, Russia/Giraudon

20 Hendrick Hondius (1573–1649), *Ferdinand II of Habsbourg*, 1634, courtesy of Topham Picturepoint/Roger-Viollet

21 artist unknown, *Ferdinand II, Holy Roman Emperor*, courtesy of Bridgeman Art Library/Kunsthistorisches Museum, Vienna, Austria

22 Diego Velázquez (1599–1660), *King Philip IV of Spain*, 1644, courtesy of Corbis © Geoffrey Clements

23 Carlo Maratti, after Van Dyck (1625–1713), *Charles I in Three Positions*, courtesy of Bridgeman Art Library © The Trustees of the Weston Park Foundation, UK

24 Polish School (17th century), *Portrait of Wladyslaw*, courtesy of Bridgeman Art Library/Wilanow Palace, Warsaw, Poland

25 after Sebastian Bourdon (1616–71), *Christina, Queen of Sweden*, 1823, courtesy of akg images

26 Jan van de Hoecke (17th century), *Emperor Ferdinand III*, courtesy of Getty Images

27 artist unknown, *Portrait of John IV of Portugal*, courtesy of Corbis © Historical Picture Archive

28 Hyacinthe Rigaud (1659–1743), *Portrait of Louis XIV*, 1701, courtesy of Topham Picturepoint/Alinari

29 Charles Le Brun (1619–90), *Portrait of Louis XIV*, *c.* 1658–1700, courtesy of Corbis © Archivo Iconografico, S.A.

30 artist unknown, *Alexis Mikailovitch*, courtesy of Topham Picturepoint/Roger-Viollet

31 artist unknown (17th century), *Ferdinand IV of Hungary*, *c.* 1654, courtesy of Getty Images

32 Daniel Jerzy Schultz (1615–83), *John II Casimir*, courtesy of Bridgeman Art Library/Musee Municipal, Cambrai, France/Giraudon

33 A. Margerstadt (17th century), *King Frederick III of Denmark and Norway*, courtesy of The Art Archive/Gripsholm Castle, Sweden/Dagli Orti

34 Abraham Wuchters (1608–82), *King Charles X Gustavus of Sweden*, courtesy of The Art Archive/Gripsholm Castle, Sweden/Dagli Orti

35 artist unknown, *Portrait of Alfonso VI of Portugal*, courtesy of Corbis © Historical Picture Archive

36 Austrian School (17th century), *Portrait of Leopold I, Holy Roman Emperor*, courtesy of Bridgeman Art Library/Heeresgeschichtliches Museum, Vienna, Austria

37 Thomas of Ypres (1617–78), *Leopold I, Holy Roman Emperor*, 1667, courtesy of Bridgeman Art Library/Kunsthistorisches Museum, Vienna, Austria

38 English School (18th century), *Charles II*, courtesy of Bridgeman Art Library/Simon Carter Gallery, Woodbridge, Suffolk, UK

39 artist unknown, *King Charles XI of Sweden*, courtesy of The Art Archive/Kalmar Castle, Sweden/Dagli Orti

40 Don Juan Carreño de Miranda (17th century), *Charles II, King of Spain*, courtesy of Corbis © Francis G. Mayer

41 artist unknown, *Portrait of Peter II of Portugal*, courtesy of Corbis © Historical Picture Archive

42 artist unknown, *Michael Wisniowiecki*, courtesy of Corbis © Historical Picture Archive

43 Justus Sustermans (1597–1681), *Christian V, as a Boy*, courtesy of The Art Archive/Palazzo Pitti, Florence/Dagli Orti

44 artist unknown (17th century), *John III, King of Poland*, courtesy of The Art Archive/Polish Institute/Eileen Tweedy

45 Russian School (17th century), *Portrait of Tsar Fyodor III Alexeevich*, courtesy of Bridgeman Art Library/Museum of Art, Serpukhov, Russia

47 J.G. Tanhauer (18th century), *Peter I in Poltava Battle*, 1710s, courtesy of Corbis © The State Russian Museum

48 circle of Sir Godfrey Kneller (1646–1723), *Portrait of James II*, courtesy of Bridgeman Art Library/Private Collection © Philip Mould Ltd, London

49 artist unknown, *Portrait of James II*, courtesy of Topham Picturepoint

50–51 William Wissing (1656–1702), *Mary II*, courtesy of Bridgeman Art Library/Scottish National Portrait Gallery, Edinburgh, Scotland

52 Sir Godfrey Kneller (1646–1723), *Portrait of William III of Orange*, courtesy of Bridgeman Art Library/Bank of England, London, UK, Photo © Heini Schneebeli

53 Michael Dahl (1656–1743), *Portrait of King Charles XII of Sweden*, *c.* 1714–17, courtesy of Bridgeman Art Library/Private Collection © Philip Mould Ltd, London

54 Louis de Silvestre (1675–1760), *Frederick Augustus II*, courtesy of Bridgeman Art Library/Gemaeldegalerie Alte Meister, Dresden, Germany © Staatliche Kunstsammlungen Dresden

55 artist unknown, *King Frederick IV*, *c.* 1730, courtesy of Getty Images

56–57 Russian School (18th century), *Portrait of Elizabeth Petrovna*, *c.* 1750, courtesy of Bridgeman Art Library/Art Gallery of Taganrog, Russia

58 artist unknown, *Philip V of Spain*, courtesy of Topham Picturepoint

59 Hyacinthe Rigaud (1659–1743), *King Philip V of Spain*, courtesy of The Art Archive/Museo del Prado, Madrid

60 Friedrich Wilhelm Weidemann (1668–1750), *Frederick I of Prussia*, *c.* 1701, courtesy of akg images

61 artist unknown, *Frederick I of Prussia*, courtesy of Topham Picturepoint/Roger-Viollet

62 Edmund Lilly (*fl.* 1702–16), *Queen Anne*, 1703, courtesy of Bridgeman Art Library/Blenheim Palace, Oxfordshire, UK

63 Polish School (18th century), *Stanislaw I Leszczynski*, courtesy of Bridgeman Art Library/Muzeum Narodowe, Warsaw, Poland, Lauros/Giraudon

64 artist unknown, *Joseph I in Coronation Robes*, 1705, courtesy of Getty Images

65 artist unknown, *Portrait of John V of Portugal*, courtesy of Corbis © Historical Picture Archive

66 Johann-Gottfried Auerbach (1697–1753), *Emperor Charles VI*, *c.* 1730, courtesy of Bridgeman Art Library/Weltliche und Geistliche Schatzkammer, Vienna, Austria

67 Antoine Pesne (1683–1757), *Frederick William I of Prussia*, 1729, courtesy of akg images

68–69 Sir Godfrey Kneller (1646–1723), *George I*, courtesy of Topham Picturepoint/World History Archive

70 studio of Charles Andre Van Loo (1705–65), *Portrait of Louis XV of France and Navarre*, 18th century, courtesy of Christie's Images Ltd

71 Swedish School, *Ulrika Eleonora, Queen of Sweden and Frederick I, King of Sweden*, *c.* 1720, courtesy of Christie's Images Ltd

71 artist unknown (1676–1751), *Frederick I, King of Sweden*, courtesy of Corbis © Bettmann

72 Arnold Boonen (1669–1729), *Portrait of Queen Catherine I of Russia*, 1717, courtesy of Christie's Images Ltd

73 Johann Heinrich Wedekind (1674–1736), *Portrait of Tsar Peter II*, 18th century, courtesy of Bridgeman Art Library/Art Museum, Samara, Russia

74 John Shackleton (*fl.* 1749–67), *Portrait of King George II*, courtesy of Christie's Images Ltd

75 artist unknown, *King George II*, courtesy of Topham Picturepoint/Print Collector/HIP

76 Louis Caravaque (1684–1754), *Portrait of the Empress Anna Ivanovna*, 1730, courtesy of Bridgeman Art Library/Tretyakov Gallery, Moscow, Russia

77 Johann Salomon Wahl (1689–1765), *King Christian VI of Denmark*, 1740, courtesy of The Art Archive/Rosenborg Castle/Dagli Orti

78–79 Nicolas De Largilliere (1656–1746), *Portrait of Frederick Augustus III*, courtesy of Christie's Images Ltd

80 Johann-Gottfried Auerbach (1697–1753), *Portrait of the Empress Maria-Theresa*, 1749, courtesy of Christie's Images Ltd

81 Antoine Pesne (1683–1757), *King Frederick II the Great of Prussia*, 1746, courtesy of Bridgeman Art Library/Schloss Augustusburg, Bruhl, Germany

82 Russian School (18th century), *Portrait of Elizabeth Petrovna*, *c.* 1750, courtesy of Bridgeman Art Library/Art Gallery of Taganrog, Russia

83 artist unknown, *Empress Elizabeth of Russia*, courtesy of Topham Picturepoint

84 Adam Friedrich Oeser (1717–99), *Portrait of Karl VII Albrecht*, courtesy of Getty Images

85 Martin Meytens II (1695–1770), *Francis I, Holy Roman Emperor*, 18th century, courtesy of Bridgeman Art Library/Kunsthistorisches Museum, Vienna, Austria

86 Antonio Gonzalez Ruiz (d. 1785), *Ferdinand VI as Patron of Arts and Sciences*, 1754, courtesy of Bridgeman Art Library/Real Academia de Bellas Artes de San Fernando, Madrid, Spain, Giraudon

87 Johann Friedrich Gerhard (*c.* 1695–1748), *Northern States Pay Homage to King Frederick V of Denmark*, 1746–66, courtesy of The Art Archive/Rosenborg Castle, Copenhagen/Dagli Orti

88 artist unknown, *Jose I, King of Portugal*, courtesy of The Art Archive/Museu Historico Nacional, Rio de Janeiro, Brazil/Dagli Orti

89 Lorenz Pasch the Younger (1733–1805), *King Adolph Frederick of Sweden*, courtesy of The Art Archive/Gripsholm Castle, Sweden/Dagli Orti

90 artist unknown, *Charles III of Spain*, courtesy of Corbis © Alinari Archives

91 William Beechey (1775–1839), *George III*, 1760, courtesy of Topham Picturepoint/World History Archive

92 Dmitrij Grigorevic Levickij, *Catherine II as Legislatress in the Temple of the Goddess of Justice*, courtesy of Corbis © The State Russian Museum

93 Alexander Roslin (1718–93), *Portrait of Catherine II*, 1776–77, courtesy of Corbis © reproduced by permission of The State Hermitage Museum, St Petersburg

94 Elisabeth Vigée-Lebrun (1755–1842), *Stanislas II Auguste Poniatowski*, 1802, courtesy of Topham Picturepoint/Roger-Viollet

95 artist unknown, *Joseph II, Holy Roman Emperor*, 18th century, courtesy of Corbis © Archivo Iconografico, S.A.

96 Jens Juel (1745–1802), *King Christian VII of Denmark*, courtesy of The Art Archive/Rosenborg Castle, Copenhagen/Dagli Orti

97 Alexandre Roslin (1718–93), *King Gustav of Sweden*, 1775, courtesy of The Art Archive/Gripsholm Castle, Sweden/Dagli Orti

98–99 Antoine-François Callet (18th century), *Portrait of Louis XVI*, 1788, courtesy of Corbis © Johansen Krause/Archivo Iconografico, S.A.

100 artist unknown, *Queen Maria I*, 18th century, courtesy of The Art Archive/Gripsholm Castle, Sweden/Dagli Orti

101 Anton Graff (1736–1813), *Frederick William II of Prussia*, 1788, courtesy of akg images

102 Francisco de Goya (1746–1828), *Carlos IV*, 1798–99, courtesy of Corbis © Archivo Iconografico, S.A.

103 Jean-Etienne Liotard (1702–89), *Leopold II, Holy Roman Emperor*, courtesy of Bridgeman Art Library/Hofburg, Vienna, Austria

104 Friedrich von Amerling (1803–87), *Emperor Francis II of Austria*, 1832, courtesy of Bridgeman Art Library/Weltliche und Geistliche Schatzkammer, Vienna, Austria

105 Johann Pasch (1752–1811), *King Gustav IV Adolph of Sweden*, courtesy of The Art Archive/Gripsholm Castle, Sweden/Dagli Orti

106 Jacques-Fabien Gautier d'Agoty (1710–81), *Portrait of the Dauphin, later King Louis XVII of France*, courtesy of Bridgeman Art Library © Private Collection, Photo © Rafael Valls Gallery, London, UK

107 artist unknown, *Paul I of Russia*, courtesy of Topham Picturepoint/Roger-Viollet

108–109 W. Herbig (1787–1861), *Frederick III, Emperor of Germany*, courtesy of Bridgeman Art Library/Apsley House, The Wellington Museum, London, UK

110–111 Joseph Stieler (1799–1856), *A Portrait of King Oscar of Sweden as Crown Prince*, 1823, courtesy of akg images © Sotheby's

112–113 Baron François-Pascal-Simon Gérard (1770–1837), *Alexander I of Russia*, courtesy of Bridgeman Art Library/Apsley House, The Wellington Museum, London, UK

114 Jacques-Louis David (1748–1825), *Napoleon on Horseback at the St Bernard Pass*, 1801, courtesy of Corbis © Archivo Iconografico, S.A.

115 French School, *Portrait of Napoleon*, courtesy of Christie's Images Ltd

116 Francisco de Goya (1746–1828), *Ferdinand VII*, 1814, courtesy of Corbis © Archivo Iconografico, S.A.

117 Vicente Lopez y Portana (1772–1850), *Ferdinand VII of Spain*, 1805, courtesy of akg images/Erich Lessing

118 Hans Hansen (1769–1821), *King Frederick VI of Denmark*, courtesy of The Art Archive/Bymuseum, Copenhagen/Dagli Orti

119 Per Krafft the Elder (1724–93), *King Charles XIII of Sweden and Norway*, 1781, courtesy of The Art Archive/Gripsholm Castle, Sweden/Dagli Orti

120 Charles Louis Acar (b. 1804), *Portrait of Willem Frederick, Prince of Orange*, 1830, courtesy of Bridgeman Art Library/Musee de l'Armee, Brussels, Belgium/Patrick Lorette

121 artist unknown, *Portrait of King Louis XVIII*, courtesy of Corbis © Archivo Iconografico, S.A.

122 Jose Luis Carvalho (18th century), *John VI, King of Portugal*, courtesy of The Art Archive/Museu Historico Nacional, Rio de Janeiro, Brazil/Dagli Orti

123 artist unknown, *King Charles XIV John of Sweden*, courtesy of The Art Archive/Gripsholm Castle, Sweden/Dagli Orti

124 Thomas Lawrence (1769–1830), *The Prince Regent, Later George IV*, courtesy of Bridgeman Art Library © Tokyo Fuji Art Museum, Tokyo, Japan

125 studio of François-Pascal-Simon Gérard (1770–1837), *Charles X, King of France*, courtesy of Topham Picturepoint/Roger-Viollet

126 artist unknown, *Tsar Nicholas I*, courtesy of Bridgeman Art Library

127 artist unknown, *Maria II, Queen of Portugal*, 1830, courtesy of The Art Archive/Museo de Arte Antiga, Lisbon/Dagli Orti

128 artist unknown, *Miguel, Prince of Portugal*, *c.* 1828, courtesy of Getty Images

129 Sir Martin Arthur Shee (1769–1850), *Portrait of King William IV*, 1833, courtesy of Corbis © Archivo Iconografico, S.A.

130–131 Horace Vernet (1789–1863), *Louis-Philippe and his Son Leaving the Château de Versailles*, 1848, courtesy of Corbis © Archivo Iconografico, S.A.

132–133 Gottlieb Bodmer (1804–1837), *King Otto of Greece in Greek National Dress*, *c.* 1835, courtesy of akg images

134 José Guttierez de la Vega (1791–1865), *Isabella II, Queen of Spain*, 1848, courtesy of akg images/Erich Lessing

135 Joseph Bayer (1804–31), *Ferdinand I of Austria*, 1831, courtesy of akg images

136 George Hayter (1792–1871), *Queen Victoria*, 1863, courtesy of the National Portrait Gallery, London

137 artist unknown, *Victoria, Queen of England*, *c.* 1887, courtesy of Topham Picturepoint/World History Archive

138 Christian Hornemann (1765–1844), *King Christian VIII of Denmark*, courtesy of The Art Archive/Rosenborg Castle, Copenhagen/Dagli Orti

139 Nicholas Pieneman (1809–60), *The Prince of Orange, later King William II of the Netherlands*, courtesy of Bridgeman Art Library/The Crown Estate

140 Franz Krueger (19th century), *Frederick William IV, King of Prussia*, *c.* 1845, courtesy of akg images

141 Joseph Stieler (1799–1856), *A Portrait of King Oscar of Sweden as Crown Prince*, 1823, courtesy of akg images © Sotheby's

142 Johan-Vilhelm Gertner (1818–71), *Frederick VII, King of Denmark*, 1861, courtesy of The Art Archive/Rosenborg Castle, Copenhagen/Dagli Orti

143 Carl von Blaas, *Kaiser Franz Josef of Austria in Uniform*, *c.* 1884, courtesy of Corbis © Fine Art Photographic Library

144 artist unknown, *William III, King of the Netherlands*, courtesy of The Art Archive/Miramare Palace, Trieste/Dagli Orti

145 Jules de Vignon (1815–85), *Portrait of Emperor Napoleon III in Coronation Robes*, courtesy of Bridgeman Art Library © The Bowes Museum, Barnard Castle, County Durham, UK

146 Photograph courtesy of Getty Images

147 artist unknown, *Alexander II, Tsar of Russia*, 19th century, courtesy of The Art Archive/Miramare Palace, Trieste/Dagli Orti

148–149 C.W. Sondels, *King Charles XV of Sweden and Norway*, courtesy of The Art Archive/Gripsholm Castle, Sweden/Dagli Orti

150 Domenico Induno (1815–78), *Victor Emanuel II*, courtesy of The Art Archive/Museo del Risorgimento Macerata/Dagli Orti

151 Photograph courtesy of Corbis © Bettmann

152 artist unknown, *Wilhelm I, King of Prussia*, courtesy of Topham Picturepoint/World History Archive

153 Gottlieb Biermann (1824–1908), *Kaiser Wilhelm I*, courtesy of Bridgeman Art Library/Historisches Museum der Stadt, Vienna, Austria

154 Johansen Krause, *Portrait of Christian IX of Denmark*, courtesy of Corbis/Johansen Krause/Archivo Iconografico, S.A.

155 Photograph courtesy of Heritage Images/The Print Collector

156 artist unknown, *Amadeus I of Spain*, *c.* 1871–73, courtesy of akg images/Erich Lessing

157 O. Bjorck, *King Oscar II Frederick of Sweden*, courtesy of The Art Archive/Gripsholm Castle, Sweden/Dagli Orti

158 José María Galván y Candela, *Portrait of Alfonso XII, King of Spain*, *c.* 1877–85, courtesy of Corbis © Archivo Iconografico, S.A.

159 Cesare Tallone (1853–1919), *Umbero I, King of Italy*, late 19th century, courtesy of akg images/Electa

160 Ivan Nikolaevich Kramskoy (1837–87), *Portrait of Emperor Alexander III*, 1886, courtesy of Bridgeman Art Library/State Russian Museum, St. Petersburg, Russia

161 Philip Alexius de Laszlo (1869–1937), *Portrait of King Alfonso XIII of Spain*, 1927, courtesy of Bridgeman Art Library/Museo de Arte Contemporáneo, Madrid, Spain/The de Laszlo Foundation

162 Bruno Heinrich Strassberger (1832–1910), *Portrait of Kaiser Wilhelm II*, courtesy of Bridgeman Art Library/Historisches Museum der Stadt, Vienna, Austria

163 Photograph courtesy of Heritage Images/The Print Collector

164 Photograph courtesy of akg images

165 Photograph courtesy of akg images

166–167 Sir (Samuel) Luke Fildes (1843–1927), *King Edward VII*, 1902, courtesy of the National Portrait Gallery, London

168 Photograph courtesy of Getty Images

169 Sir (Samuel) Luke Fildes (1843–1927), *King Edward VII*, 1902, courtesy of the National Portrait Gallery, London

170 Photograph courtesy of Corbis

171 Photograph courtesy of Corbis © Hulton-Deutsch Collection

172 artist unknown, *King Gustav V Adolph of Sweden*, courtesy of The Art Archive/Gripsholm Castle, Sweden/Dagli Orti

173 artist unknown, *Manuel II, King of Portugal*, courtesy of The Art Archive/Private Collection/Marc Charmet

174 Sir Arthur Stockdale Cope (1857–1940), *King George V*, courtesy of Bridgeman Art Library/The Crown Estate

175 Photograph courtesy of Corbis © Bettmann

176 Photograph courtesy of Corbis © Hulton-Deutsch Collection

177 artist unknown, *Emperor Karl I*, *c.* 1910, courtesy of Getty Images

178 Photograph courtesy of Topham Picturepoint

179 Photograph courtesy of Corbis © Hulton-Deutsch Collection

180 Vandyk (*fl.* 1882–1943), *Prince Edward, Duke of Windsor*, *c.* 1936, courtesy of the National Portrait Gallery, London

181 Sir Gerald Kelly (1879–1972), *King George VI*, *c.* 1941, courtesy of the National Portrait Gallery, London, copyright reserved

182 Photograph courtesy of Topham Picturepoint/Roger-Viollet

183 Photograph courtesy of Corbis © Bettmann

184 Photograph courtesy of Corbis © Bettmann

185 Photograoh courtesy of Corbis © Bettmann

186 Pietro Annigoni (1910–88), *Queen Elizabeth II*, 1969, courtesy of the National Portrait Gallery, London

187 Photograph courtesy of Corbis © Bettmann

188 Photograph courtesy of Corbis/Selwyn Tait

189 Photograph courtesy of Topham Picturepoint/Polfoto

190–191 Photograph courtesy of akg images/NordicPhotos

192 Photograph courtesy of Topham Picturepoint

193 Photograph courtesy of D. Virgili and published with permission of His Majesty the King of Spain's Household

194 Photograph courtesy of the Netherlands Government Information Service (RVD)

195 Photograph courtesy of Corbis © Tim Graham

Index

Page numbers in **bold** indicate main entries;
page numbers in *italics* indicate illustrations.

A Crown

Issued in 1679

A Guinea

Issued in 1719

A Sixpence

Issued in 1893

A Euro

Issued in 2002